FRONTLINES

Equipping Christian Leaders to Respond to Adolescent and Young Adult MENTAL HEALTH ISSUES

Kevin Van Lant, Ph.D.
Laura Wingard, MA, LMFT
CIFT Equip

Table of Contents

CIFT Equip, Publisher
Kevin Van Lant, Editor
Laura Wingard, Associate Editor
Laura Pasquale, Copy Editor
Shauna Wagoner, Graphics Designer
Vanessa Mendozzi, Cover Artist

ISBN 978-1-7354192-0-6 (paperback)
ISBN 978-1-7354192-1-3 (ebook)

1633 E. Fourth St., Suite 120, Santa Ana, CA 92701

Preface—Addressing the Need for Information and Training

The purpose of this manual is to accompany in-person training that will equip youth pastors, lay leaders and educators to assess and triage common adolescent and young adult mental health issues. Christian youth leaders and educators are often on the interpersonal frontlines of our current mental health crisis, and so are in need of more information on the care and triaging of those suffering from mental illness. This is particularly important because many of those in your care will typically consult with youth pastors, teachers and lay leaders ***before*** seeking care from a mental health professional. Furthermore, because more than 50% of all chronic mental illness manifests prior to age 14, youth pastors, educators and lay leaders are in a unique position that allows them to intervene in the early stages of someone's mental health journey, possibly mitigating future suffering.

Although this aspect of your ministry role may at times seem somewhat daunting, it is also an opportunity to make a lasting, positive impact! With this book and through training, it is our goal to equip you with language and tools to respond with compassion and knowledge to those who are suffering with mental health issues. To do this, ***Frontlines*** training will:

i. Normalize and destigmatize mental illness.
ii. Guide participants in overcoming their own anxieties related to engaging someone with a mental illness.
iii. Equip participants with resources, knowledge and language to better engage those who are suffering.
iv. Emphasize a uniquely Christian perspective on attending to those with mental health concerns.
v. Encourage a broader Christian community response when possible and appropriate.

Upon completing the Frontlines training, you will be able to triage common mental health concerns experienced by those in your care. This will be accomplished by learning the 5-point *Frontlines* triaging approach we refer to as "**LASER**": Listen - Assess - Strategize - Explore - Refer.

i. LISTEN for key words that suggest someone may be struggling with a mental health concern.
ii. ASSESS the type and severity of the mental health issue presented.
iii. STRATEGIZE a potential response to the mental health concern.
iv. EXPLORE potential options with the afflicted individual as well as the accessibility and openness to these options.
v. REFER to appropriate mental health professionals when necessary.

Acknowledgements

The concept for this manual and accompanying in-person training were simply that, a concept, until the CIFT board of directors encouraged and supported the actualization of this project. I would like to thank the CIFT board of directors and CIFT leadership for their vision and desire to better support those who are working on the Frontlines of Christian ministry and Christian education, attending to the very real psychological and spiritual needs of those who are in their care. I would also like to thank those who supported this project with their financial and logistical support. It could not have happened without your willingness to fund this fledgling project. Additionally, I am grateful for Laura Wingard's editorial assistance. Your willingness to share from your experiences with adolescents and young adults as a therapist and former youth pastor have been invaluable. To the contributing authors I am grateful for the opportunity to work on another project with you. This has been a delight for me. I would like to thank Shauna Wagoner for her remarkable publication layout abilities. The readability and style of this manual are a complete testament to your remarkable skills. And lastly, I'd like to express my gratitude for the copy-editing assistance of Laura Pasquale. Your professionalism, thoughtfulness and comprehensive feedback have been greatly appreciated.

— Kevin Van Lant, Ph.D.

IMAGE SOURCE: Pixabay

"Mental pain is less dramatic than physical pain, but it is more common and also more hard to bear. The frequent attempt to conceal mental pain increases the burden: it is easier to say, 'My tooth is aching' than to say, 'My heart is broken.'"

— C.S. Lewis

Kevin Van Lant, Ph.D.

Introduction to the Nature of the Mental Health Crisis among Adolescents and Young Adults and the Role of the Christian Community

The Scope of America's Mental Health Crisis

The United States is currently experiencing a mental health crisis. Although this crisis appears to include nearly every age, race and gender category, adolescents and young adults appear to be particularly impacted (see Figure 1). Although we might assume youth to be a time of growth and simple joys, adolescents and younger adults experience a surprisingly high incidence of mental illness, with almost one in four experiencing a major depressive episode during high school, and approximately 32% of 13- to 18-year-olds reporting symptoms of clinical levels of anxiety at some point during their adolescence. Moreover, many mental illness conditions commonly occur together. Data from the Center for Disease Control (CDC, 2020) indicate that three out of four children and adolescents 3- to 17-years-old who experience depression also have anxiety (73.8%), and that almost half have a significant behavior problem (47.2%). Of those suffering with mental illness, less than half receive *any* form of treatment (43.1%), with Caucasian Americans pursuing treatment at the highest rate (48.7%) and Asian Americans at the lowest rate (21.6%). Reasons for avoiding treatment can range from lack of available services, cultural prohibitions against discussing problems with persons outside the family, economic hardship, fear of parental censure or even punishment, language barriers, and other obstacles.

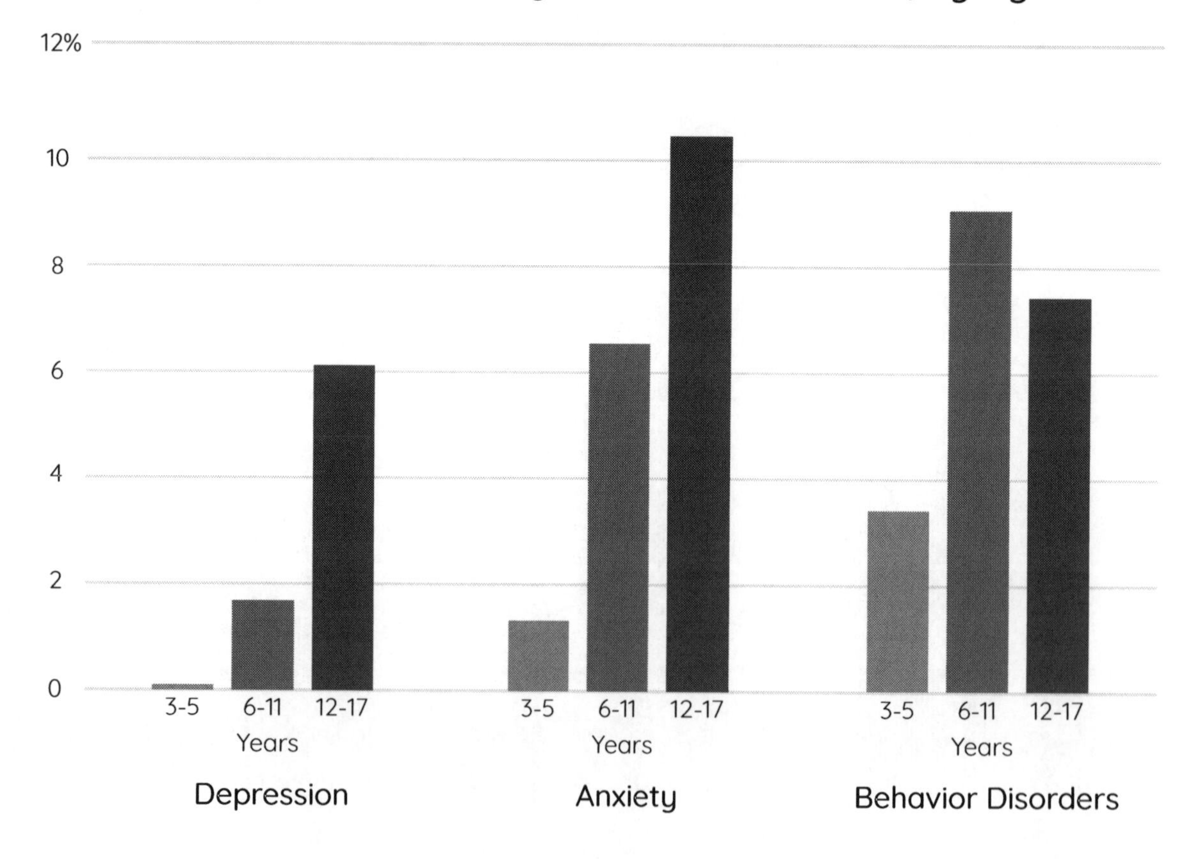

Figure 1
Incidence of Mental Health Issues Among Adolescents

SOURCE: SAMHSA

Suicide rates have received considerable attention both within the mental health community and in the culture at large. Suicide is the second leading cause of death among 10- to 34-year-olds, the fourth leading cause of death among 35- to 54-year-olds, and the tenth leading cause of death in the U.S. population overall (NIMH, 2019).

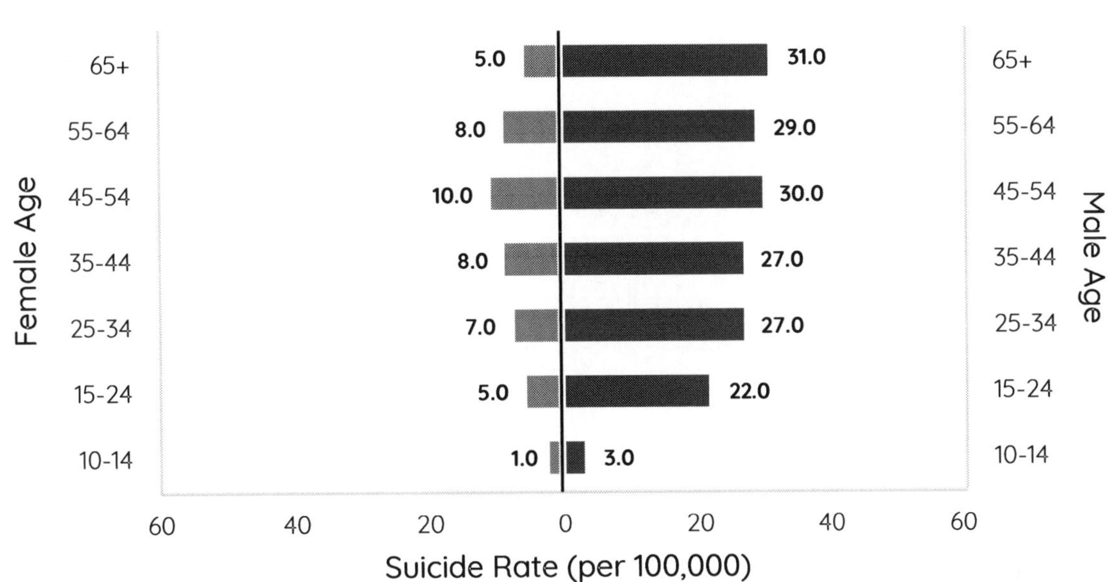

Figure 2
Suicide Rates by Age in the U.S.

SOURCE: NIMH, 2019

Suicide rates have also increased significantly among nearly every demographic group, representing a 26% increase overall between 1999 and 2016. More recently, so called "deaths of despair" (suicide and drug and alcohol overdose) have reached an extraordinary level, with certain counties in the U.S. reporting an increase of nearly 600% (Woolf, S. & Schoomaker, H., 2019). As of this writing, the rates of these deaths have reduced the mean life expectancy in the U.S. for four years in a row, contributing to the first decrease in life expectancy since the Spanish Flu pandemic of the early twentieth century.

What Do the Terms "Mental Health" and "Mental Illness" Actually Mean?

The terms "mental health" and "mental illness" are frequently used by the general public interchangeably and with little exact definition. Perhaps this is due to disagreement regarding exactly what each may mean, as well as the historical stigma attached to the term "mental illness." Throughout this manual we will attempt to delineate what we mean by "mental health" and "mental illness", recognizing that they both lie on the *continuum* of human experience, rather than an either/or characterization of mental health or mental illness. Also, it's important to remember that an individual who is functioning normally today might find herself or himself challenged by a disorder in the future. In that sense, there is no such thing as "the mentally ill", a negatively charged term, largely rejected by practitioners, which doesn't reflect the reality of health and illness, and seems to send the destructive message that one group carries the burden of illness while all others—"the rest of us"—are somehow immune.

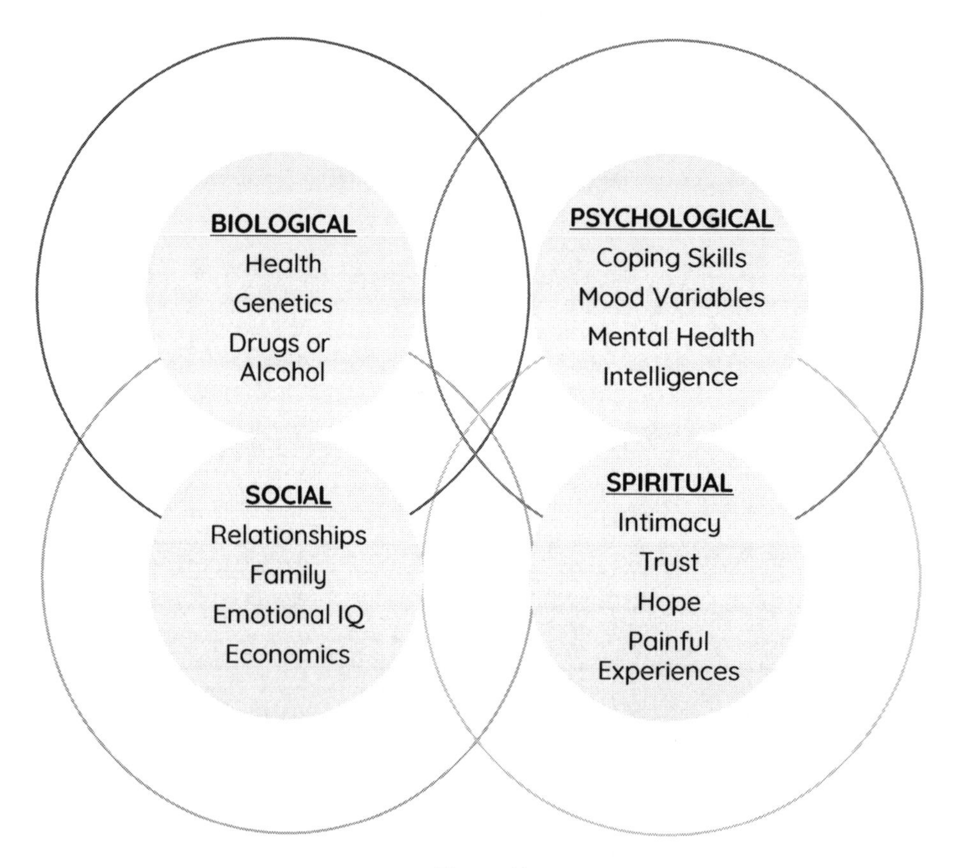

Figure 3
Biopsychosocialspiritual Model

(Van Lant, 2020)

For example, a person who has recently lost a loved one and is steeped in deep grief may manifest many of the same symptoms as someone who is experiencing clinical depression. However, we would not necessarily refer to that bereaved individual as "depressed"; that diagnosis would require a specific set and duration of symptoms. Instead, it's very likely that the individual is doing the hard—but healthy—work of grieving and letting go. His or her mental health is being impacted by normal psychological processes, biological predispositions, and relational losses, as well as their experience of God. Therefore, consistent with that example, this manual will espouse a "biopsychosocialspiritual" model of what it means to be human, and how each of these four components interact with our psychological well-being or lack thereof.

Mental Illness and the "4 D's"

During the past century, mental illness has been largely defined by the criteria found in the *American Psychiatric Association's Diagnostic and Statistical Manual for Mental Disorders (Fifth Edition)* (DSM-5). The DSM-5 describes various symptoms, syndromes, and diagnostic criteria for nearly every known mental disorder. Although our manual will generally attempt to avoid technical diagnostic language, the four components that are frequently addressed in detail within the DSM-5, and that commonly define mental illness, are the "4 D's": deviance, dysfunction, distress and danger (Comer, 2017).

Deviance	Deviance from typical, statistical or cultural norm
Dysfunction	A disturbance, deficiency or impairment of function or behavior
Distress	Unpleasant feelings or emotions that impact one's level of functioning
Danger	Danger to oneself or others

Table 1
Comer's "4 D's" of Mental Illness (2017)

Deviance represents the degree to which an individual varies from normative behavior and thought processes. It's important to remember that an individual's behaviors and thought processes are often culturally defined, and, therefore, cultural context needs to be considered when evaluating mental health. (Consider, for example, what would be perceived as normal for a 17-year-old female living in a Northeastern inner city versus a 71-year-old male living on a rural farm).

Dysfunction refers to the individual's lack of capacity to function in a situationally normative manner. This may include such things as their ability to work, attend school, or even address such basic self-care behaviors as showering, preparing food, or brushing their teeth.

The person's subjective level of ***distress*** is a key component of mental health and mental illness. Typically, a person will define his or her psychological functioning in terms of the degree to which he or she is *experiencing* emotional suffering and distress, as opposed to what others might observe. For example, a person with Bipolar Disorder, who is experiencing a manic episode, might be unaware of their own distress or level of functioning, or of the suffering they might be causing loved ones or those around them, due to their euphoria.

Danger refers to the degree to which an individual is having suicidal or homicidal thoughts. A substantial portion of this manual will be dedicated to assessing and responding to a person who may be experiencing such suicidal ideation.

Taking a positive stance, as "Image Bearers" of God, Christians believe that human beings reflect God's nature in a variety of ways, one of which is God's capacity to feel. The Bible is filled with descriptive examples of God's emotionality. We are broken, however, and can feel the effects of both personal and corporate sin; therefore, our emotionality is an imperfect and partial reflection of God's image, though still an essential aspect of being human. Because our emotional experiences are intertwined with every other aspect of life, mental health and/or mental illness, too, will nearly always be fully or partially defined by one's unique emotional process. So, when we talk about mental health and mental illness, we are talking about various aspects of the whole person, and not just a diagnosis.

The Role of the Christian Community

The church, as well as what we think of as the broader Christian community, have both played a historically vital role in responding to the mental health needs of those in its care. Scripture tells us that we have an obligation to care for those in need, and for those who are suffering (see, for instance, 2Corinthians 1:3-7, Matthew 25:34-40, and so on). The Christian tradition of charity, as well as a practical Christian theology, would suggest that caring for those who suffer physically or psychologically is a form of redemptive care. Although the church's historical response to those with mental illness has not been consistently humane or biblical, the works of such individuals as Cotton Mather, Dorthea Dix, and Karl Menninger, who were motivated by a sense of Christian charity, were instrumental in changing the ways in which we treated chronically mentally ill persons. These examples can be looked upon with great pride, as demonstrating how Christians can influence an entire culture for good.

More recently, the U.S.-based church in particular has seen a developing openness to develop better systems and capacities to attend to the those in their congregations who might be suffering as a result of mental illness (Smietana, 2014). Historically, many denominations have founded or operated clinics and hospitals to provide physical health care. And today, churches such as Saddleback Church in Orange County, California, and Woodlands Church in Texas have devoted significant resources and staff toward developing and maintaining sizable mental health-oriented care ministries. Although ministries of this size might be unattainable for many church communities, it is possible for even the smallest church to focus deliberate attention toward those with mental health concerns, and to do so in a manner that is supportive, destigmatizing, and meaningful for the entire church community.

Be Prepared

Individual churches and parachurch organizations can respond in a variety of ways to adolescents and young adults in their communities who are suffering with mental health concerns. To do this, however, the church must be prepared. The first step toward such preparation is to signal that congregants can bring their mental health concerns to those in ministry, either directly or in the context of pastoral counseling. Research suggests that almost two thirds of those who struggle with mental health issues and have a church affiliation will consult with their pastor or ministry leader prior to seeking professional care. Therefore, the ability to assess what's being presented, and to differentiate between relatively typical life situations with congruent emotions and cognitions, as opposed to more clinical-type needs that would benefit from professional intervention, is a key aspect of "being prepared."

One aspect of preparation may involve priming your youth ministry community by openly talking about mental health-related issues on a regular basis. This may take place in contexts as varied as middle school and high school church gatherings or leadership trainings to small groups. This process of education and normalization of emotional and psychological suffering, as evidenced both in scripture and day-to-day life experiences, may be instrumental in beginning to destigmatize symptoms of mental illness. Finally, consider how you might set limits on your ministry, too, so that referrals will be made to link persons with necessary professional services. Timely referrals will free up energy to work with more congregants and not to burn out in the process.

Mental Health-Oriented Care Ministries for Adolescents and Young Adults

It's vital that ministry leaders begin to think of care ministries within their churches as a form of mental health ministry. Nearly all care ministries are oriented toward the well-being, flourishing, connection and growth of congregants. These are core aspects of mental health and, when missing from a person's life, can exacerbate or even cause various forms of mental illness such as depression and anxiety. Care ministries such as the Landing (Celebrate Recovery for students), DC4K (DivorceCare for Kids) and smaller mental health-oriented affinity groups each minister to the emotional and relational needs of participants and attend to each component of their biological, psychological, social and spiritual lives.

Types of Care Ministries	Target Audience
The Landing - Celebrate Recovery for Students	Education and affinity-oriented recovery groups for nearly all mental health issues
DivorceCare for Kids	For children of divorcing parents

Types of Care Ministries	Target Audience
GriefShare	For those who have experienced the loss of a loved one
Small Groups for those Experiencing Depression or Anxiety	Small groups for those who are or have struggled with these disorders
NAMI Small Group	Education and support for those who have family members with mental illness

Table 2
Type of Care Ministries and Their Target Audiences

(Van Lant, 2020)

Interestingly, 68% of pastors recently stated that their churches already provide certain types of mental health resources, yet *fewer than 28% of congregants were aware of these resources* (Smietana, 2014). This suggests that youth pastors, churches, and ministry leaders could improve the degree to which they communicate about the types of mental health resources being offered, as well as more actively connecting those who may be suffering with mental health issues, both to provide these resources and to do so in a way that is impactful for their communities.

Take the story of Monica, for example. During a Wednesday night youth group series on the Psalms, her youth pastor read the following verses: "I am worn out from groaning. All night long I flood my bed with weeping and drench my couch in tears. My eyes grow weak with sorrow; they fail because of all my foes." (Psalm 6:6-7, NIV). Her youth pastor suggested that in fact David may have been struggling with depression as he wrote this Psalm, and that some students in the youth ministry may at times feel something similar.

As Monica heard this, she began to weep and sought prayer when the gathering concluded. The youth leader who prayed with Monica suggested that she consider meeting with the youth pastor for counseling and perhaps discuss her feelings with her recently divorced mother. The youth pastor was able to counsel Monica later that week, and determined that she had been struggling with depression and anxiety since the separation of her parents several months earlier. She was then able to meet with Monica and her mother and gave Monica a referral to a local Christian therapist, recommending that she consider participating in the church's newly launched *Landing* ministry.

The youth pastor's willingness to describe Monica's battle with depressive symptoms during the Wednesday night message (education and normalization), to hear Monica's degree of emotional suffering (listening), and to provide the appropriate resources enabled Monica to begin to heal from her battle with depression and anxiety (referral). This encounter later resulting in facilitating a *Landing* small group for others suffering from depression (community impact).

Who Should be Trained to Triage Possible Mental Health Issues?

The extent to which one should be trained to triage mental health issues may very well depend on the degree to which they interact with the general public and with those within their church or organizational community. Since most students who attend a church will interact first with their youth pastor or lay leader regarding mental health concerns, it's imperative that youth pastors and church leadership are equipped to triage such issues, as those issues relate to the students as well their family members.

Young adult mental illness rates have risen significantly over the past several years. Recent data suggests that nearly 50% of all mental illness presents by age 14, and 75% presents by age 21 (World Health Organization, 2020). Since early intervention can lessen the severity of future mental illness symptomatology, youth pastor awareness and intervention can be a key factor in improving a young adult's psychological and relational future.

Parachurch organizations are frequently confronted with many of the same issues that arise in church contexts. That said, campus ministry leaders, youth camp leaders, missions organizations and educators would each benefit from our *Frontlines* training. Each of these ministries is in frequent direct contact with students, and is confronting the unique mental health needs of their staff and constituencies, including those in need of further support and assessment.

Necessity of Early Intervention and Benefits for the Entire Church Community

The documented benefits of early intervention are numerous. As mentioned previously, early intervention in most mental illness situations may decrease the severity and complexity of later symptoms, as well as of other, potential co-existing conditions (Hetrick, et al., 2016). For example, depression prevention programs positively correlate with (in other words, "have been found to lead to") a reduction in depression diagnoses, symptomatology, and rate of hospitalizations. In addition, early intervention and prevention programs clearly benefit the individual receiving support, and also reduce the potential for family disruption.

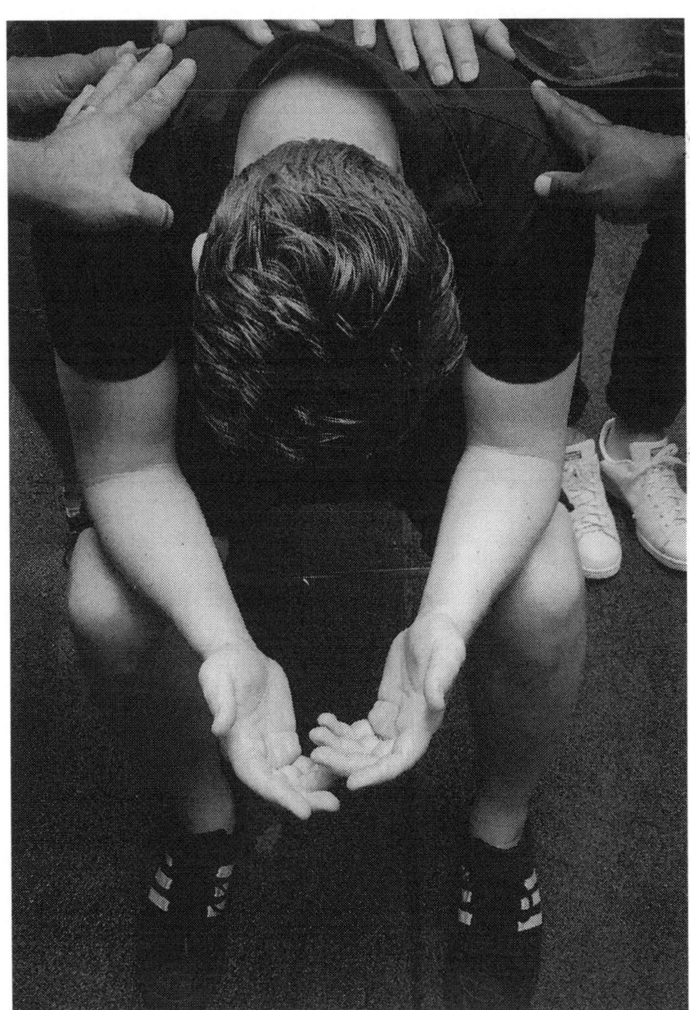
IMAGE SOURCE: Unsplash

Early intervention and triage by ministry leaders can also benefit the entire church family. Church and parachurch ministries that provide care, support, and appropriate resourcing and referral can be a source of grace and mercy that conveys the historical value of Christian charity as well as a reflection of Christ's embodied love. As scripture tells us, "If one part suffers, all the parts suffer with it, and if one part is honored, all parts are glad" (1 Corinthians 12:26, NLT).

When symptoms are addressed, the individual and the entire group can experience relief and rejuvenation. Attending to the mental health needs of your students, staff and others in your care is ultimately a form of care for your entire church community.

Lastly, the development of mental health-oriented care ministries and attentiveness to the mental health needs of your church community may also result in surprising evangelistic opportunities. Care ministries, such as the Landing, GriefShare, mental health-oriented affinity groups, DivorceCare for Kids, etc., not only meet the needs of your students, but also meet the needs of unchurched members of your broader community. Those who might be reluctant to attend a youth service on a weekend, for instance, might be more open to an invitation by a friend to visit a care ministry that they perceive to acknowledge their very real emotional needs.

Application of Handbook Content to an Adolescent and Young Adult Population

This chapter presented recent statistics to underscore the urgency of the need for mental health awareness and for the availability of services in our communities. To close, we'll focus on specific highlights for those in ministry.

Important Take-Aways for Ministry Leaders

- Mental illness rates in the U.S. have increased significantly over the last 15 years.
- Suicide is the second leading cause of death for persons between 10 and 34 years old.
- Mental health-oriented care ministries can meet an important need within youth ministries.
- It's important to remember that each individual should be seen as a whole person, having biological, psychological, social and spiritual aspects of his or her being.
- The "4 D's" of mental illness are deviance, distress, dysfunction, and danger.
- Nearly 50% of all mental illness presents by age 14, and 75% of cases become evident by age 21.
- Approximately 67% of those who attend church and struggle with mental health issues will consult with their pastor prior to seeking help from a mental health professional.

RESOURCES

Online Organizations and Support:

National Alliance on Mental Illness: https://www.nami.org

United Way 211: A virtual service to connect individuals to support.
https://www.211unitedway.org

Books:

Moreland, J.P. (2019), ***Finding quiet: My story of overcoming anxiety and the practices that brought peace.*** Grand Rapids, MI: Zondervan. ISBN-10: 031059720X ISBN-13: 978-0310597209

Van Lant & Bettenhausen (2019), ***Counseling and Mental Health in the Church: The Role of Pastors and the Ministry.*** San Diego, CA: Cognella. ISBN-10: 1516528255 ISBN-13: 978-1516528257

Stafford, M.S. (2017), ***Grace for the Afflicted: A Clinical and Biblical Perspective on Mental Illness.*** Downers Grove, IL: IVP. ISBN-10: 0830845070 ISBN-13: 978-0830845071

Apps:

(Note: These are examples, not endorsements by the author.)

Moodpath: Depression & Anxiety by MindDoc Health GmbH

Sanvello for Stress & Anxiety: Sanvello Health, Inc.

Moodnotes: Mood & CBT Tracker: ThrivePort, LLC

UCLA Mindful App

REFERENCES

Center for Disease Control. (2020). ***Data and Statistics on Children's Mental Health.*** https://www.cdc.gov/childrensmentalhealth/data.html

Comer, R.J., & Comer, J.S. (2017). ***Abnormal psychology (10th ed.),*** New York, NY: Worth Publishers.

Hetrick, S.E., Cox, G.R., Witt, K.G., Bir, J.J., & Merry, S.N. (2016). Cognitive behavioural therapy (CBT), third-wave CBT and interpersonal therapy (IPT) based interventions for preventing depression in children and adolescents. ***Cochrane Database of Systematic Reviews, 8***, Art. no: CD003380. doi:10.1002/14651858.CD003380.pub4.

National Institute of Mental Health (2019). ***Mental Illness.*** https://www.nimh.nih.gov/health/statistics/mental-illness.shtml

National Institute of Mental Health (2019). ***Suicide.*** https://www.nimh.nih.gov/health/statistics/suicide.shtml

Smietana, B. (2014). ***Mental illness remains taboo topic for many pastors.*** https://lifewayresearch.com/2014/09/22/mental-illness-remains-taboo-topic-for-many-pastors/

Woolf, S., & Schoomaker, H. (2019). Life expectancy and mortality rates in the United States, 1959-2017. ***Journal of the American Medical Association, 322***(20), 1996-2016. doi: 10.1001/jama.2019.16932.

World Health Organization (2020). ***Child and adolescent mental health.*** https://www.who.int/mental_health/maternal-child/child_adolescent/en/

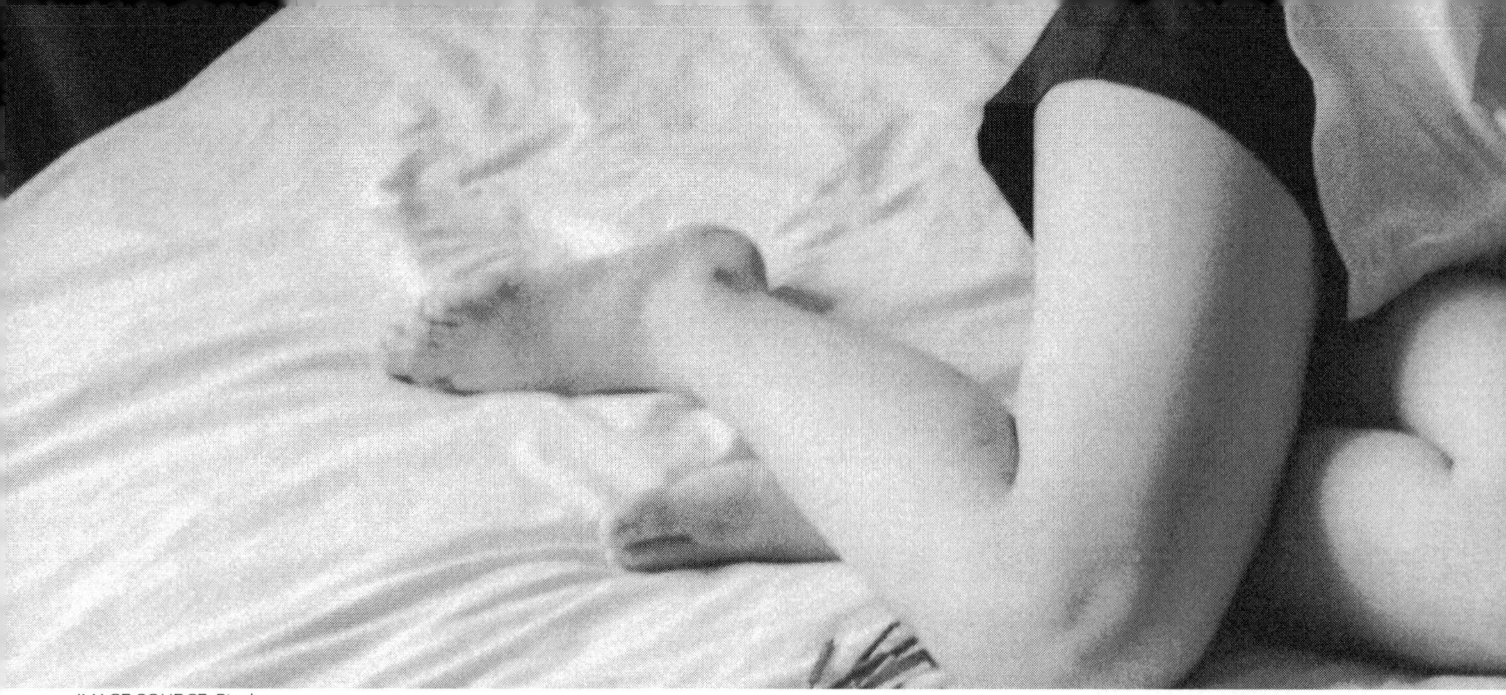

IMAGE SOURCE: Pixabay

"I've told you all this so that trusting me, you will be unshakable and assured, deeply at peace. In this godless world you will continue to experience difficulties. But take heart! I've conquered the world."

— John 16:33

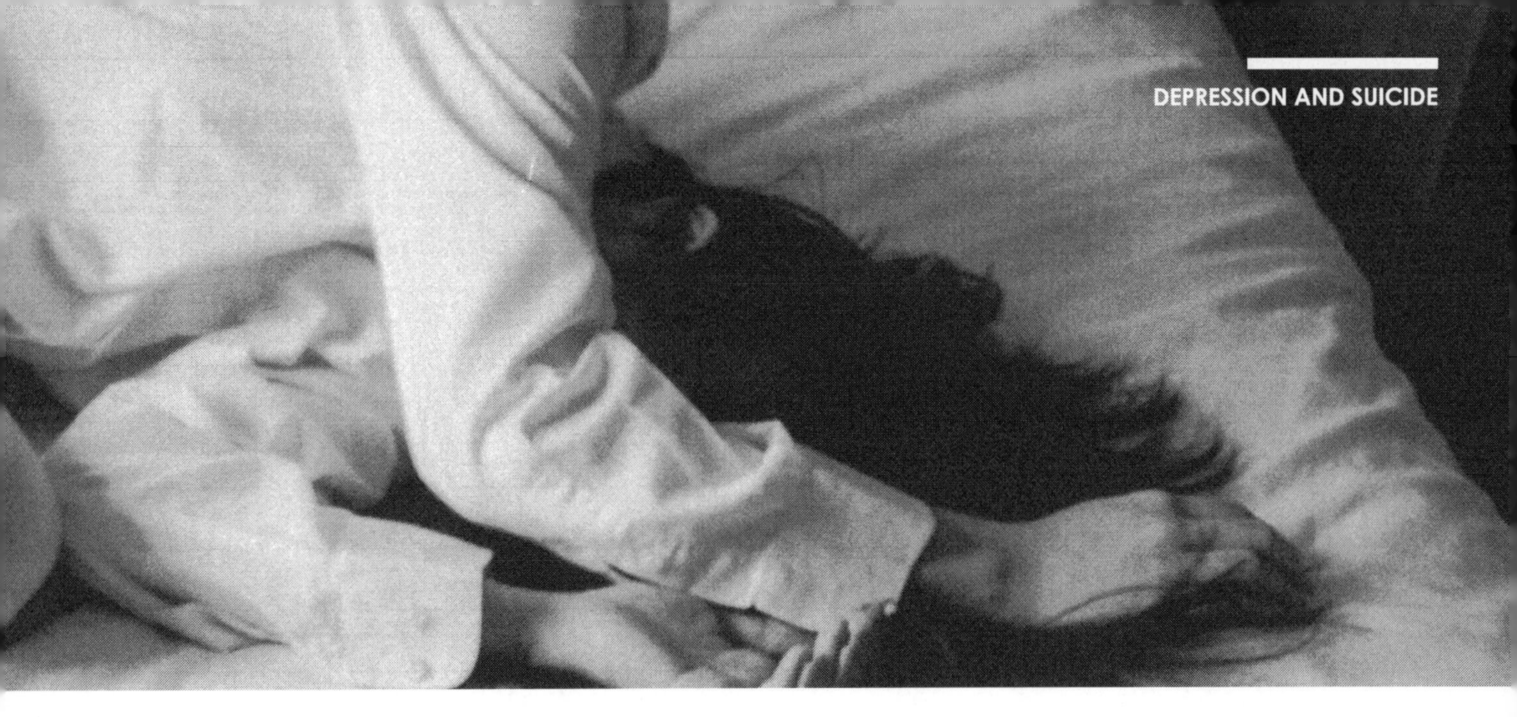

Jaclyn Yorkey, LMFT
Laura Wingard, MA, LMFT

Adolescent and Young Adult Depression

The Nature of Adolescent and Young Adult Depression

To say the least, being a young person (ages 10 to 25) is complex and difficult. With extensive hormonal and neurological changes constantly causing changes in mood, it can be very hard to differentiate between normal sadness and a possible depressive disorder. While ups and down are normal and typically more frequent in young people, when a young person has been overwhelmed and sad for an extensive period of time, it may become a cause for concern.

When a young person is faced with a stressful situation, adults must remember that this may be the first time he or she is trying to navigate a set of complex feelings. Adaptive coping skills are learned over time with healthy modeling, counsel and advice from the healthy people in their lives. Young people have limited coping skills to address feelings of sadness and, in some situations, they may only know how to mimic the maladaptive coping mechanisms modeled by the adults in their lives. Thus, in adolescence, emotional resources may be limited and, if unaddressed, over time can foster more serious disorders like depression. If a young person is facing deep emotional pain, pain that is not processed and adapted to in healthy ways, changes in mood that last several weeks to months may be the first signal of a depressive disorder.

A ***depressive disorder*** is a mental illness which affects all aspects of daily functioning: sleeping, eating, school, sports, relationships, motivation, etc. (we will discuss these in depth later in the chapter). This illness can happen at any age, but symptoms typically first develop in early teenage years. The early development of symptoms and the value of early intervention are why it is so important to notice the beginning signs of depression, and to be able to differentiate between normal ups and downs of adolescence from the early signs of depression. If young people and the adults around them have more psychoeducation on the symptoms of depressive disorders, then these symptoms can be caught and treated early in life. This will lead to not only a healthier adolescence but also a healthier adulthood. Clinical depression is a highly treatable illness, and with swift intervention, depression can be stabilized through psychotherapy and medication, when necessary.

An example of depression commonly seen in therapy may actually be quite difficult to differentiate from the stereotypical attitudes seen in young people: moody, agitated, sleepy, fickle, hungry and all around emotional. While this may be true in some young people (due to dramatic hormonal changes, navigating relationships for the first time, possible family and academic stress, etc.), there are very straightforward ways to notice if these symptoms are a cause for concern.

The first signal is a *lasting change in behavior*, especially if it follows a new stressor. For example, if a young person begins high school (facing extreme social stress, struggling academically, body image issues, family stresses, etc.), and one month later, a once jovial disposition changes to consistently agitated, and he or she begins to isolate, this is a cause for concern and needs to be immediately addressed. The second signal is *how long these new behaviors last.* If this same student simply needs time to adjust and proper guidance on how to manage the new stressors in high school, these symptoms will dissipate naturally. But, with no intervention, they may get worse, lasting weeks to months, and possibly triggering depression.

A constant concern when ministering to depressed adolescents is ***suicidal ideation***, that is, thinking about, considering or planning suicide. It is very common for clinically depressed individuals to experience extreme feelings of despair, loneliness and hopelessness that may lead to thoughts of suicide. When depression begins to feel increasingly more despairing, with no perceived way out, death may feel like the only viable escape from overwhelming sadness. Suicidal thoughts are often more about ending the emotional pain rather than desiring actual death. Death, therefore, seems like the only way to end the pain. Some young people may have thoughts of suicide, but have no actual intent to end their lives, because suicidal thoughts are much different than an actual plan to end one's life. For other young people, though, thoughts of suicide are accompanied with intent and a plan to end their lives.

Although suicidality is not always present with symptoms of major depression, it is important to remember that suicidal individuals are almost always struggling with some form of depression, and that assessing ***suicidal intent*** can be complex and difficult. Therefore, this manual will attempt to provide information that may be helpful in assessing risk, and when to report suicide, as well as instructions on how to refer these individuals for professional intervention.

Types of Depression

If a professional diagnosis has been made, the following terms are often used:

Major Depressive Disorder (MDD) This disorder is characterized by:

- Sad feelings most of the day, nearly every day for at least two consecutive weeks
- Experience a loss of interest or pleasure in activities (such as socializing, sports, hobbies) that were once meaningful
- Weight gain or loss
- Fatigue, sleep disturbances
- Feelings of worthlessness, difficulty concentrating
- Thoughts of death

Persistent Depressive Disorder (PDD) This disorder is characterized by:

- Typically feels depressed most of the day, for more days than not, for at least 2 years
- PDD includes most symptoms seen in MDD, with the notable exception of suicidal thoughts and feelings.
- Those with PDD may experience relief from their symptoms for up to 2 months at a time.

Bipolar I, Bipolar II, or Cyclothymia This disorder is characterized by:

- Depression that fluctuations between manic or hypomanic episodes
  - **Manic** episodes involve excessive happiness or irritability, high levels of activity or fixation on a goal, decreased need for sleep, pressured speech, distractibility, and greater involvement in dangerous behavior.
  - **Hypomanic** episodes are similar to manic episodes, but with less severe symptoms and a shorter duration. (Please see the chapter on psychosis for more information on Bipolar I and II Disorders.)

The specific causes of depression are highly variable and multifaceted. A combination of internal and external factors is nearly always at play. Consider a 19-year-old male who is struggling to find meaningful relationships during his first years in college. With growing isolation, perhaps a growing distance from family and church support, and memories of similar feelings of loneliness earlier in his life, these circumstances may cause him to seek relief using alcohol or other drugs. Consistent with our biopsychosocialspiritual model of mental illness, all of these factors combined may result in a diagnosis of major depression, rather than the presence of only one issue. This is the case for many people who experience significant depressive symptoms: some combination of environment and biology interact in a complex manner, with no single cause or solution.

The Data

As we see in Figure 1, an estimated 3.2 million adolescents ages 12 to 17 reported at least one major depressive episode in 2017. We also see that depression impacts individuals of every race, gender, age, and economic standing. The prevalence of diagnosed depression is highest among women, among people aged 18 to 25, and among those who self-identify as belonging to two or more racial groups.

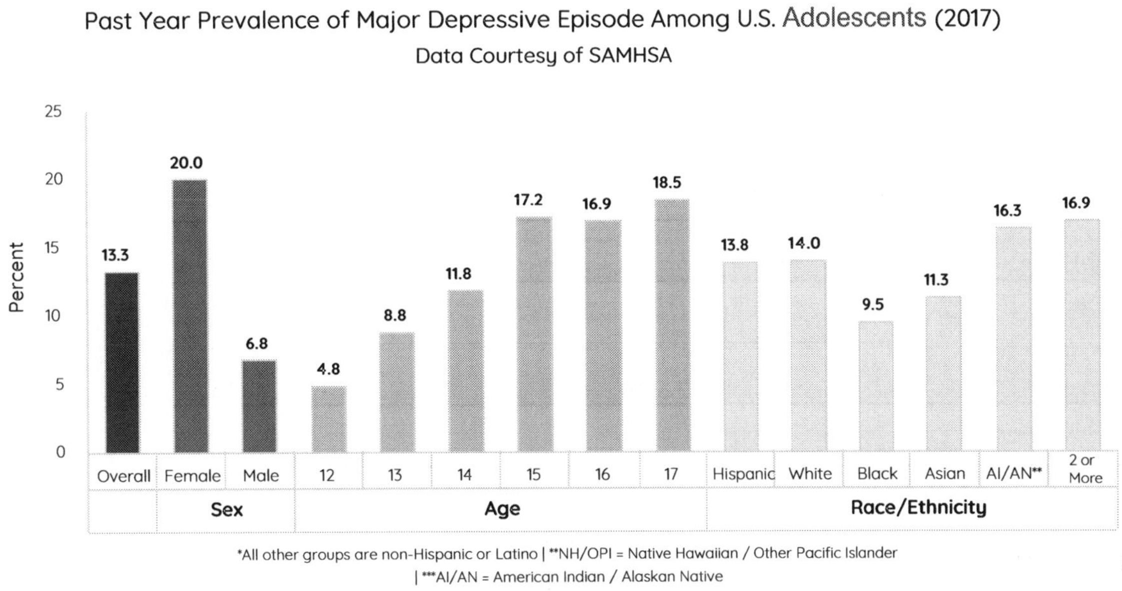

Figure 1
Demographic Data on Major Depression Among Adolescents, 2017

SOURCE: https://www.nimh.nih.gov/health/statistics/major-depression.shtml

Next, as we see in Figure 2, more than 60% of adolescents go without treatment. Yet, as we already know, depression is one of the most treatable mental illnesses. Lack of treatment may be due to widespread inability to identify the actual symptoms of depression in young people. (Others may not seek treatment due to denial, fear of stigma, lack of access or affordability, mistrust of practitioners, and so on.) As people age and experience symptoms of depression for longer periods of time, these symptoms are easier to identify and more likely to result in seeking and finding successful treatment.

As Figure 2 also indicates, psychotherapy and medication are typical treatments for depression. Although some adolescents may be treated with medication only, this is not the preferred approach and tends to have a relatively low success rate. High rates of success are found with either psychotherapy alone, or with a combination of psychotherapy and medications when necessary. While a discussion regarding the use of antidepressant medications with young people is complex, it should be noted that there is a lack of significant data regarding the long-term effects of psychotropic medication on a young person's brain, which is still developing rapidly at their stage of life. Therefore, many therapists are likely to establish other forms of treatment *before* referring to a psychiatrist for medication.

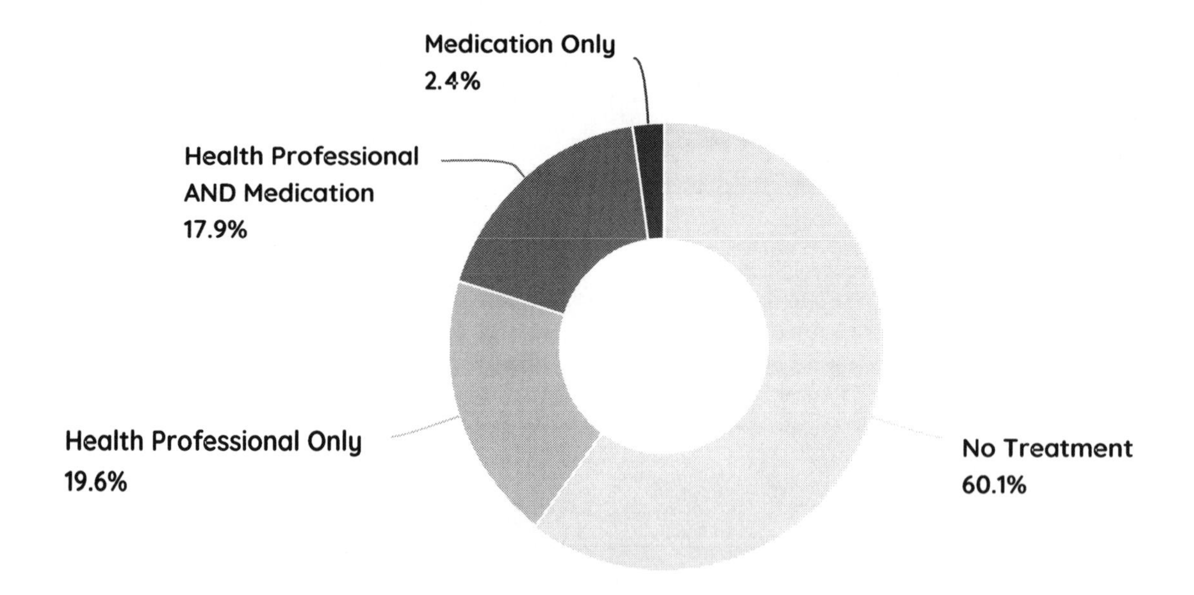

Figure 2
Data on Depression Treatment Approaches, 2017

SOURCE: https://www.nimh.nih.gov/health/statistics/major-depression.shtml

What are the Common Symptoms of Adolescent Depression?

Below is a list of possible symptoms. Many of these symptoms can be experienced within each type of diagnosed depression.

Physical:

- Low energy
- Fatigue
- Sleep disturbances: insomnia and/or hypersomnia
- Increased or decreased appetite
- Headaches
- Chronic pain

Psychological:

- Aggression, agitation: *This is important an distinguishing factor in young people as opposed to adults.*
- Difficulty making decisions
- Poor Concentration
- Low self-esteem
- Hopelessness
- Guilt
- Self-reproach
- Loneliness
- Feeling empty
- Feelings of despair
- Feelings of worthlessness
- Concurrent anxiety

Social:

- Isolation from others
- Avoidance of others
- Lack of motivation to move towards others
- Lack of engagement in activities with others
- Difficulty engaging in pleasurable experiences
- Feeling unable to relate to others
- Sexual identity issues

Spiritual:

- Lack of meaning and purpose
- Insecurity and self-doubt
- Guilt and shame
- Feelings of worthlessness relative to God
- Doubt
- Apathy

Red Flags for Depression

Working in ministry, we might not be able to observe all of the causes and symptoms listed. So what are the most *likely* red flags for depression and suicide?

- Marked changes in sleep patterns
- Lack of proper hygiene (consider what is normal for the person's age and income level)
- Withdrawal and isolating behavior (for example, avoiding conversation)
- Decrease in normal activities (doesn't show up for youth group or other functions)
- Difficulty going to work or school
- Making comments such as "I don't feel myself lately." or "I feel empty inside."
- Expressing sadness for no identifiable reason
- Difficulty paying attention

According to the National Alliance on Mental Illness (NAMI, 2010), the following questions are appropriate to ask the young person or someone in the young person's inner circle (family, friends, teachers, etc.) when assessing a young person for a possible depressive disorder:

- Do you constantly feel sad, anxious, or even "empty," like you feel nothing?
- Do you feel hopeless or like everything is going wrong?
- Do you feel like you're worthless or helpless? Do you feel guilty about things?
- Do you feel irritable much of the time?
- Do you find yourself spending more time alone and withdrawing from friends and family?
- Are your grades dropping?
- Have you lost interest or pleasure in activities and hobbies that you used to enjoy?
- Have your eating or sleeping habits changed (eating or sleeping more than usual or less than usual)?
- Do you always feel tired? Like you have less energy than normal, or no energy at all?
- Do you feel restless or have trouble sitting still?
- Do you feel like you have trouble concentrating, remembering information, or making decisions?

- Do you have aches or pains, headaches, cramps, or stomach problems without a clear cause?
- Do you ever think about dying or suicide? Have you ever tried to harm yourself?

Risk Factors for Developing a Depressive Disorder

The causes of depression are varied and include a range of overlapping possibilities. As one can imagine, it can be difficult to determine the exact cause of depression for any given individual. As with the other disorders presented in this manual, depression can be caused by both external and internal factors. ***External depression*** is reactive, triggered by an outside stimulus, such as burnout, stress, family strain, relational distress, trauma, or grief. ***Internal depression*** is considered to be biochemically caused, or endogenous, as shown by lower levels of serotonin, rapidly changing hormones, or chronic illness that directly impacts mood. Often, depression may be the result of a combination of external factors along with the biochemical factors that create a susceptibility to those stresses.

Possible external triggers of depression include:

- School-related stress and burnout
- Worry about family members
- Ruptures in relationships
- Stress and burnout related to academics
- Rapidly changing hormones (puberty)
- Unresolvable stress
- Guilt
- Chronic illness
- Traumatic events (whether personal or involving a larger group)
- Loss of a loved one
- Loss of something important
- Abuse by those inside or outside the home (whether emotional, mental, sexual physical, and whether chronic or sudden)
- Fear of previous depression reoccurring
- Sexual identity issues

Suicide

Not all depressed persons are suicidal, however, these are some of the red flags for that specific symptom:

- Statements such as "Death would be a relief", and, "There is no point in living anymore."
- Giving away belongings
- Saying "goodbyes"
- Excessive alcohol and/or drug use (as opposed to experiment use common in young people)
- Prior attempts
- Hearing voices
- Recent loss of support system (such as church, employment, family, friends, intimate relationship)
- Terminal illness
- Sexual identity issues

Recent research shows concerning trends in the data on suicide. For example, in 2018, the total number of suicides in the U.S. was 48,344. This number is alarming, in that it represents the highest national rate of suicide in 50 years. In addition, between 2001 and 2017, the total suicide rate in the US increased by 31%. After unintentional injury, the *leading cause of death* in those between 10 to 34 years of age is suicide (see Figures 3 and 4).

Leading Causes of Death in the United States (2016) Data Courtesy of CDC								
	Select Age Groups							
Rank	10-14	15-24	25-34	35-44	45-54	55-64	65+	All Ages
1	Unintentional Injury 847	Unintentional Injury 13,895	Unintentional Injury 23,984	Unintentional Injury 20,975	Malignant Neoplasms 41,291	Malignant Neoplasms 116,364	Heart Disease 507,118	Heart Disease 635,260
2	**Suicide 436**	**Suicide 5,723**	**Suicide 7,366**	Malignant Neoplasms 10,903	Heart Disease 34,027	Heart Disease 78,610	Malignant Neoplasms 422,927	Malignant Neoplasms 598,038
3	Malignant Neoplasms 431	Homicide 5,172	Homicide 5,376	Heart Disease 10,477	Unintentional Injury 23,377	Unintentional Injury 21,860	CLRD 131,002	Unintentional Injury 161,374
4	Homicide 147	Malignant Neoplasms 1,431	Malignant Neoplasms 3,791	**Suicide 7,030**	**Suicide 8,437**	CLRD 17,810	Cerebro-vascular 121,630	CLRD 154,596
5	Congenital Anomalies 146	Heart Disease 949	Heart Disease 3,445	Homicide 3,369	Liver Disease 8,364	Diabetes Mellitus 14,251	Alzheimer's Disease 114,883	Cerebro-vascular 142,142
6	Heart Disease 111	Congenital Anomalies 388	Liver Disease 925	Liver Disease 2,851	Diabetes Mellitus 6,267	Liver Disease 13,448	Diabetes Mellitus 56,452	Alzheimer's Disease 116,103
7	CLRD 75	Diabetes Mellitus 211	Diabetes Mellitus 792	Diabetes Mellitus 2,049	Cerebro-vascular 5,353	Cerebro-vascular 12,310	Unintentional Injury 53,141	Diabetes Mellitus 80,058
8	Cerebro-vascular 50	CLRD 206	Cerebro-vascular 575	Cerebro-vascular 1,851	CLRD 4,307	**Suicide 7,759**	Influenza & Pneumonia 42,479	Influenza & Pneumonia 51,537
9	Influenza & Pneumonia 39	Influenza & Pneumonia 189	HIV 546	HIV 971	Septicemia 2,472	Septicemia 5,941	Nephritis 41,095	Nephritis 50,046
10	Septicemia 31	Complicated Pregnancy 184	Complicated Pregnancy 472	Septicemia 897	Homicide 2,152	Nephritis 5,650	Septicemia 30,405	**Suicide 44,965**

Figure 3

Leading causes of death (2016 data)

SOURCE: https://www.nimh.nih.gov/health/statistics/suicide.shtml

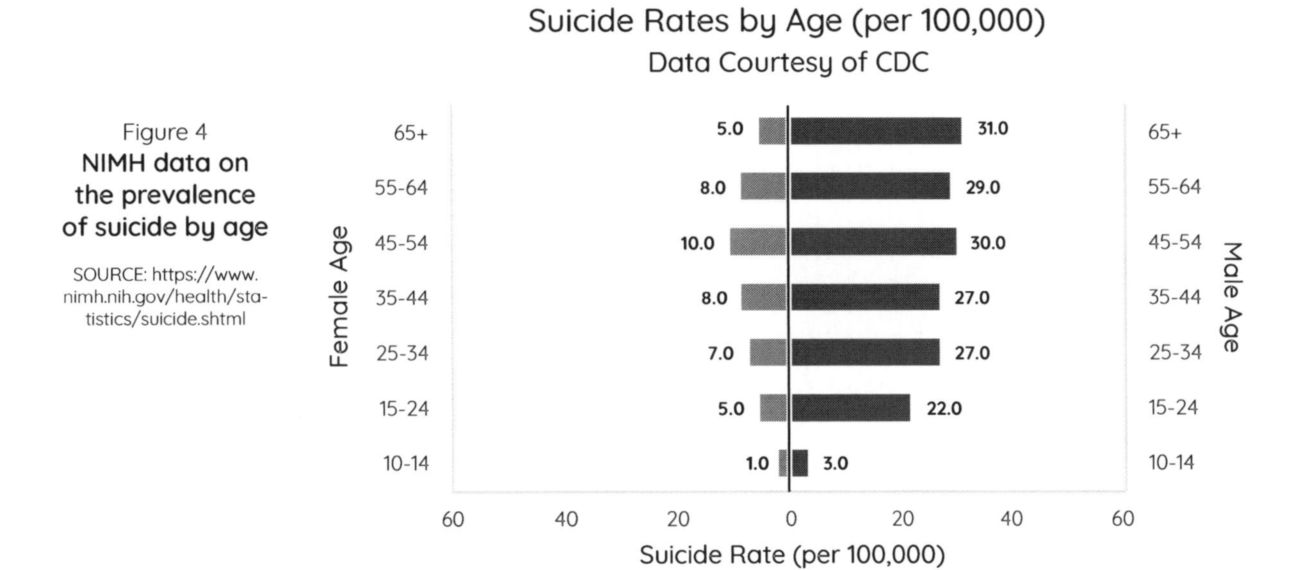

Figure 4

NIMH data on the prevalence of suicide by age

SOURCE: https://www.nimh.nih.gov/health/statistics/suicide.shtml

Demographic Differences

As Figure 5 indicates, race and ethnicity are associated with differing rates of suicide. Although it is beyond the scope of this manual to explore the many racial factors affecting suicide rates, it is important for ministry leaders to know that Native Americans and White Non-Hispanics currently experience a disproportionally high suicide rate, as documented extensively during recent decades. This should be considered when assessing for depression or suicide risk.

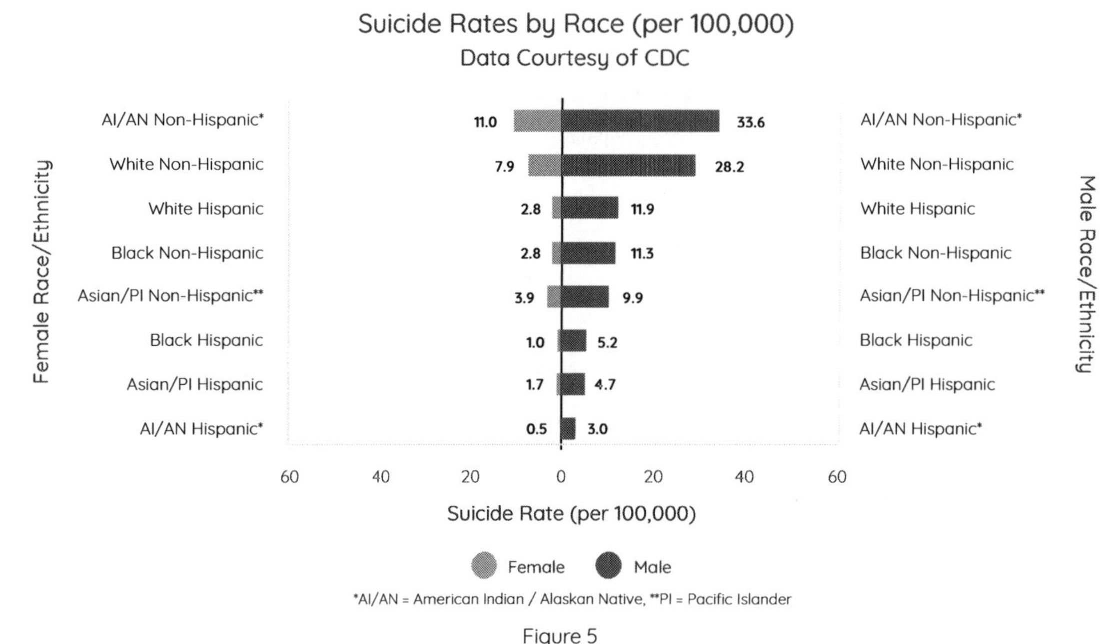

Figure 5
Prevalence of suicide among racial and ethnic groups in the U.S.

SOURCE: https://www.nimh.nih.gov/health/statistics/suicide.shtml

Suicidal thoughts and intentions expressed by those in our care can be among the most frightening, disempowering and confusing of all ministry scenarios. It is important, therefore, to discuss any reported or suspected suicidal intent, plans or thoughts with your direct supervisor or a trusted colleague. Because all suicidal thoughts need to be addressed with great care, consultation with experienced ministry leaders and/or with available mental health professionals should be sought, both to add insight and direction and to support the individual providing ministry during a potentially stressful time.

An assessment for suicide is a complex task that should generally be handled by mental health professionals. That said, Juhnke's (1994) "SAD PERSONS" suicide assessment protocol can be a helpful tool when talking with someone who seems to be expressing suicidal thoughts. The SAD PERSONS scoring system should only be considered a loose guide for determining suicidal potential, and not as the whole picture, as many individuals may act upon suicidal thoughts even when experiencing very few of indicators in this scale.

It is important to remember that asking individuals about their possible intent to harm themselves will not increase their risk or likelihood that they will do so, or that they will take their own lives. In fact, the opposite tends to be true. People who are considering suicide may actually find some relief from these thoughts by talking them through with an empathetic and caring person in their lives. Moreover, by initiating such a difficult conversation, you may very well be the first person to make space for them to talk about the degree of suffering they may be experiencing, giving you an opportunity to assist them in getting the care they so desperately need.

SAD PERSONS Suicide Assessment Items

Sex: Men have a higher likelihood of committing suicide.
Age: Individuals over 65 years of age have an elevated risk.
Depression: Clinical depression increases the chance of committing suicide by 20%
Prior History: Prior attempt may be the best indicator that another attempt will be made.
Ethanol Use: Alcohol and drug use increases the risk of attempting/ completing suicide.
Rational Thinking Loss: Psychosis (disorientation, hearing voices, etc.) increases risk of attempts.
Support System Loss: Loss of an important attachment figure by separation or death.
Organized Plan: Having a plan to commit suicide increases the risk of committing suicide.
No Significant Other: Lack of support due to loss, isolation, or negligence.
Sickness: Terminal illness increases the risk of suicide by 20%.
Scoring system: 1 point for each positive answer above.

Score/Risk

Score	Risk
0 - 2	Refer to counseling services; person allowed to go home.
3 - 4	Encourage counseling services, then follow up closely; evaluate need for hospitalization.
5 - 6	Consider hospitalization, voluntarily or involuntarily, depending on level of trust that the individual will return for another meeting.
7 - 8	Hospitalize.

Figure 6
SAD PERSONS Assessment Items

(Juhnke, 1994)

While the final risk category in the SAD PERSONS assessment indicates hospitalization, this is not something that most youth pastors or ministry leaders are trained to coordinate on their own. Therefore, in the case of involuntary hospital admission in particular, reaching out to first responders or to trained mental health professionals is essential.

What to Do When a Young Person is Expressing Suicidal Thoughts or Intent

Pastors, who are legally considered to be mandated reporters, are required to intervene when they suspect someone is a danger to themselves. The responsibility of suicide reporting can create a lot of fear and anxiety for most ministry workers. However, the church is typically a safe place for young people to share the depth of the pain they are feeling, and it is very common for a young person to report to a pastor or small group leader that he or she is considering suicide. While many youth workers are trained in how to respond in this circumstance, many are not, and they may not know that it is essential to intervene when a young person expresses suicidal ideation.

IMAGE SOURCE: Pixabay

If a young person reports suicidal ideation to anyone other than the mandated reporter (who could be a pastor, director, staff member of the church), this non-mandated reporter (typically a volunteer leader) should only feel responsible to report this to the pastor or to a direct supervisor.

When a young person shares suicidal thoughts the best steps to take are as follows:

1. *If the threat is immediate:* call 911 or take the young person to a local hospital emergency room.
2. If a young person shares suicidal ideation with a *volunteer* or *with non-church staff*:
   a. It is *essential* to inform the young person that the volunteer is *obligated* to tell someone immediately.
   b. Ideally, the young person and volunteer will collaborate on how to immediately involve the pastor.
   c. It is highly advised not to keep this information a secret, even if the young person resists sharing it with trusted persons.
   d. The volunteer should strive not to relay this sensitive information without the consent and collaboration of the young person, *unless it is necessary* (that is, unless the young person refuses to grant permission to tell a supervisor, in which case the volunteer must share the information, even without explicit permission).
3. If the young person or the volunteer shares this information with a pastor, the young person and the pastor should collaborate on how to involve parents or guardians immediately:
   a. Ideally, the pastor and parents collaborate on next steps (based on severity):
      i. Set an appointment with a mental health professional ASAP
      ii. Remove any lethal means of suicide from home
      iii. Provide 24 supervision
      iv. Seek immediate hospitalization

The 4 D's of Mental Illness

Let's summarize the information in this chapter using the 4 D's.

Deviance—How might a young person's symptoms differ from what one would normally expect to see under similar circumstances?

____

____

Dysfunction—How might a young person's experience of the disorder(s) potentially interfere with their ability to function in day-to-day life (e.g., school, social, etc.)?

____

____

Distress—Describe the biopsychosocialspiritual distress that might be associated with the disorder(s).

____

____

Danger —What types of words or actions might suggest that the person you're interacting with is in some type of danger?

____

____

LASER

Now, use the LASER to evaluate the experiences and possible responses suggesting a more serious mental health concern.

for key words that suggest someone may be struggling with a mental health condition

ASSESS

the type and severity of the mental health issue presented

STRATEGIZE

to develop a potential response to the mental health concern

EXPLORE

potential interventions with the afflicted individual as well as the accessibility and openness to these options

REFER

to appropriate mental health professionals when necessary

LISTEN

LISTEN for key words that suggest someone may be struggling with a mental health condition

LASER-focus for Depression

- I feel sad all the time.
- I want to cry most of the time.
- I feel guilty about everything.
- I'm unlovable.
- No one would care if I was no longer around.
- I don't want to get out of bed.
- Life feels overwhelming and difficult.
- I haven't been myself for a while.
- I feel empty and hollow inside.
- I can't think clearly.
- I'm angry all of the time (especially common in depressed young people).

NOTES:

ASSESS the type and severity of the mental health issue presented

ASSESS

LASER-focus for Depression

- Determine if the sadness expressed takes place daily and how long it has been experienced.
- Is the sadness or depression disrupting their ability to go to work or school?
- Is their depression disrupting their normal sleeping and eating habits?
- Are they withdrawing from friends and family?
- Have they lost interest in doing things that once brought them joy?
- Do their thoughts seem clouded?

NOTES:

STRATEGIZE

STRATEGIZE to develop a potential response to the mental health concern

LASER-focus for Depression

- Review strategies the person has considered and/or tried in the past, in order to determine what was helpful or unhelpful and why.
- Because research has shown that burnout can lead to depression, evaluate current life commitments, including stresses that can be eliminated or reduced for the time being.
- When was the last time they had a physical examination and testing of thyroid function?
- Explore the possibility of utilizing computer or cell phone apps, such as *Moodpath* or *Mood Meter*, to assist in giving language to feelings as well as helpful strategies for coping.
- Collaborate about who would be a caring, safe person for them to connect with on a regular basis (friend, pastor, therapist).

NOTES:

EXPLORE potential interventions with the afflicted individual as well as the accessibility and openness to these options

EXPLORE

LASER-focus for Depression

- Evaluate interventions and potential barriers to carrying out suicidal plans.
- Exercise has been shown to release feel-good endorphins. Discuss the possibility for integrating this into their day.
- Diet has been shown to have an impact on depression. Explore ways to increase healthy food input, reducing caffeine, junk food, and sugar consumption.
- Consider community groups and resources the person would be open to in their faith communities. (If no list is available, contact United Way 2-1-1 online.)
- Discuss potential care ministries available within the church community (e.g., Celebrate Recovery; small groups oriented toward mental health; Youth DivorceCare).

NOTES:

REFER

REFER to appropriate mental health professionals when necessary

Laser-focus for Depression

- Psychologists (Ph.D., PsyD), licensed clinical social workers (LCSW), and marriage and family therapists (MFTs) are appropriate referrals for treating depression.
- Therapists may refer to a psychiatrist for a psychiatric consultation and possible medication.
- Physicians are appropriate referrals for medical examinations (young people need to have thyroid evaluated).
- Nutritionists may be another appropriate referral for medical evaluations and consultation about nutritional deficiencies.
- Online support groups, such as the Depression and Bipolar Support Alliance (DBSA), may be helpful and supportive.

NOTES:

LISTEN for key words that suggest someone may be struggling with a mental health condition

LASER-focus for Suicidality

- There's no point in living anymore.
- I can't see a way out of my sadness.
- Death would be a relief.
- I just don't want to be here anymore.
- Life is meaningless and there isn't any hope for my future.
- I just want to be done.
- I can't keep doing this.
- If anything happens to me, promise to take care of _____.
- I want to disappear.
- I don't think I'll be at school/work/church next week.

NOTES:

ASSESS

ASSESS the type and severity of the mental health issue presented

LASER-focus for Suicidality

- Determine if someone is considering harming themselves by *directly* asking if they are thinking about it or planning it.
- If they mention having a plan, ask questions about their method and how accessible it would be for them. (The more specific and complete the responses, the greater the reason for concern.)
- Do they have a history of attempting suicide?
- Do they regularly drink or do drugs?
- Consider using the SAD PERSONS assessment.

NOTES:

STRATEGIZE to develop a potential response to the mental health concern

STRATEGIZE

LASER-focus for Suicidality

- Openly engage in conversation with the person to offer a sense of hope and support in this time of distress.
- Collaborate on who they can trust as a safe resource to openly discuss their suicidal thoughts.
- Does this person have consistent people in their life to help monitor their well-being?
- Are they willing to reach out for help to a trusted friend, pastor, or therapist?

NOTES:

EXPLORE

EXPLORE potential interventions with the afflicted individual as well as the accessibility and openness to these options

Laser-focus for Suicidality

- Ask if the person would consider going to a local hospital emergency room to be evaluated, if he or she expresses feeling suicidal.
- Provide the person with suicide hotline numbers.
- Help them set up a plan of action to address their suicidality.
- Discuss options for treatment (for example, psychotherapy, medication, group therapy).

NOTES:

REFER to appropriate mental health professionals when necessary

REFER

Laser-focus for Suicidality

- Should someone in your ministry context discuss suicidal thoughts or feelings, and especially if they show signs of burnout, you should contact your supervisor or team leader as soon as possible.
- Psychologists (Ph.D., PsyD), licensed clinical social workers (LCSW), and marriage and family therapists (MFTs) are all appropriate referrals to someone who has suicidal thoughts or plans.
- If someone has a plan to harm themselves in the near future, consider accompanying them to the local emergency room for an emergency evaluation (sometimes referred to as a "5150 evaluation").
- If the situation is urgent, call 911 or a mobile mental health crisis unit.

NOTES:

Important Take-Aways for Ministry Leaders

- Depression affects young people and their families. Simply stated, depression is experienced as feeling hollowed out, empty, or having a complete absence of feeling. This is different from normal grief and situational sadness, which involve having distinct feelings or reactions to a life experience and expressing them. It also includes losing interest in activities that were once meaningful.

- Depression comes in different forms, such as: Major Depressive Disorder, Persistent Depressive Disorder, Seasonal Affective Disorder, Postpartum Depression, and Bipolar Disorder.

- Suicidal thoughts and/or attempts *always* need to be taken seriously and attended to. Talking about suicide is one of the best ways to prevent it. Sitting with someone, asking sincere questions, conveying messages of hope, and aiding them in getting the help they need will be critically important.

- Depression is very treatable. There are many resources that can be helpful to a person suffering with depression. Psychologists, licensed clinical social workers, marriage and family therapists, psychiatrists, physicians, naturopaths, in-person or online support groups, and faith-based community groups are all valuable resources. Multiple professionals or supports can collaborate for the care of a depressed individual.

- Unlike adults, young people may present as angry and agitated rather than sad or depressed.

RESOURCES

Online Organizations and Support:

National Alliance on Mental Health, What Families Need to Know About Teen Depression: https://www.nami.org/getattachment/Press-Media/Press-Releases/2010/NAMI-Releases-Family-Guide-on-Adolescent-Depressio/FamilyGuide2010.pdf

National Alliance on Mental Illness: https://www.nami.org

National Institute of Mental Health: https://www.nimh.nih.gov

National Association for Suicide Prevention: iasp.info

Depression and Bipolar Alliance: dbsalliance.org

United Way 211: A virtual service to connect individuals to support. https://www.211unitedway.org

National Suicide Prevention Hotline: 800-273-8255

National Youth Crisis Hotline: 800-448-4663

National Hopeline Network: 800-784-2433

LGBTQ+: It Gets Better Project: Hope for LGBT Youth (https://itgetsbetter.org) or The Trevor Project (https://www.thetrevorproject.org)

Grace Alliance: https://mentalhealthgracealliance.org

Mental Health and the Church: https://churchandmentalhealth.com

Videos:

A collection of TED Talks on the topic of suicide: https://www.ted.com/topics/suicide

13 Reasons Why (Netflix series): provides great exposure to issues/what teens are watching but is not recommended as example in successful approach to teen suicide

For Teachers: ***The Fight Against Teen Suicide Begins in Classroom:*** https://www.youtube.com/watch?v=ofjRnIpXBF0

Teen Suicide "WHY": https://www.youtube.com/watch?v=nP_xXPvJctI

Mark Yarhouse: ***Gender Identity & Faith:*** https://www.youtube.com/watch?v=K2cpwy0-fkU

Books and Digital Media:

Brown, Brenee (2010). ***The gifts of imperfection: Let go of who you think you're supposed to be and embrace who you are.*** Center City, MN: Hazelden Publishing. ISBN: 978-59285-849-1.

Fuller Youth Institute (2020). ***How to talk to any young person: An intergenerational conversation toolkit.*** Available at https://shop.fulleryouthinstitute.org/collections/leader-resources

Piper, John (2006). ***When darkness will not lift: Doing what we can while we wait for God—and joy.*** Wheaton, IL: Crossway Book. ISBN-10: 1-58134-876-2.

Schab, Lisa M. (2008). ***Beyond the blues: A workbook to help teens overcome depression.*** Oakland, CA: Raincoast Books. ISBN-10: 1-57224-611-9.

Yarhouse, Mark (2013). ***Understanding sexual Identity: A resource for youth ministry.*** Grand Rapids, MN: Zondervan. ISBN-10: 0310516188 ISBN-13: 978-0310516187

Apps:

(Note: These are examples, not endorsements by the author.)

Mood Meter by Emotionally Intelligent Schools, LLC

- This app helps to expand emotional vocabulary, discover emotional nuances, and offers strategies to help regulate feelings.

Moodpath: Depression & Anxiety by MindDoc Health GmbH

- This app helps assess emotional and physical wellbeing, track patterns and triggers, and offers techniques to improve emotional well-being.

Headspace: Mindfulness and meditation

- This app teaching mindfulness and meditation techniques proven to improve mood.

REFERENCES

Juhnke, G.E. (1994) SAD PERSONS scale review. ***Measurement & Evaluation in Counseling & Development***, 27,(1) 325.

Leonard B. E. (2010). The concept of depression as a dysfunction of the immune system. ***Current Immunology Reviews,*** 6(3), 205–212. https://doi.org/10.2174/157339510791823835

National Institute of Mental Health (2020). ***Depression.*** https://www.nimh.nih.gov/health/statistics/major-depression.shtml

National Institute of Mental Health (2020). ***Suicide.*** https://www.nimh.nih.gov/health/statistics/suicide.shtml

IMAGE SOURCE: Shutterstock (Standard License)

"Cast all your anxiety on him, because he cares for you."

— 1 Peter 5:7

Kevin Van Lant, Ph.D.
Laura Wingard, MA, LMFT

Adolescent Anxiety and Stress

The Nature of Anxiety and Stress

From a physiological perspective, adolescent stress and anxiety can look very similar to adult stress and anxiety. Similar to adults, adolescents are equipped with a biological survival system. What some psychologists refer to as our "primal brain" has always been hardwired to respond to *real* and *perceived* threats in very specific and nonconscious ways. You have probably heard these reactions commonly referred to as *flight, fight,* or *freeze* responses. Two others, *fainting* and *fawning*, have shown up more recently in domestic violence and trauma literature.

Our fear response energizes us to take action to resolve problems and to keep ourselves and others safe, including
moving away from a threat (flight), or

- addressing the threat head on (fight),
- staying still and quickly evaluating our options (freeze),
- losing consciousness when psychologically or physically overwhelmed by a situation or an actual injury (fainting), or,
- focusing on what is being demanded by others rather than on self-protection (fawning).

While each of these responses is very different, the mind and body are working together to keep the individual safe, whether through conscious decision-making and action or by unconscious mechanisms.

Adolescents, as well as adults, might even have more than one response to the same situation. The threat could be physical, like encountering a hungry bear, or it could be emotional, like an unexpected text from someone you have recently had a conflict with. It's important to remember that the responses of our primitive brain may vary based on the level of real or perceived threat, and that each individual's response will be different. We cannot assume, if someone is not "running" or avoiding a situation, that the individual feels completely comfortable or safe, or is exaggerating an experience of fear.

Many of the same biological systems that are activated when we feel fear are also activated when we feel anxiety and stress. Sometimes these emotional and biological experiences can become so intertwined that the distinction between the fear of a real threat and anxiety-provoking concern about a less distinct *possibility* can become confused or vague. In the tension between these two responses, however, we need these emotional and physical signals to tell us that something in our life is problematic and needs attention.

Often adolescents try to ignore these signals because they are unsure of what to do with the emotions, which can then result in an increasing intensity of the very feelings or circumstances that they're trying to avoid. Conversely, others may ruminate or obsess on these anxious thoughts and feelings, often in an attempt to feel that they have some control or power over them. Such typical responses can become problematic, however, when a person experiences such severe anxiety that it starts to interfere with aspects of their daily functioning such as relationships, school, sports, work, or family life.

Although anxiety and stress can feel very similar—and are terms that are often used interchangeably—it's helpful to remember that they are, in fact, quite distinct experiences. The primary difference between anxiety and stress is that ***stress*** comes from some *external* demand or factor that often can be addressed and resolved. In contrast, ***anxiety*** is the *internal* state, or a way that we cope with stress. Anxiety is our *response* when we believe that our concerns cannot can be resolved, or that we lack the resources to address them. Sometimes, even if the situation is corrected, a person may continue to experience anxiety; when that anxiety persists beyond the situation that provoked it, it may become an emotional disorder.

It's difficult to discuss adolescents without taking a brief look at adolescent brain development. The dramatic changes in the brain between ages 12 to 24 can further complicate the healthy management of anxiety and stress for adolescents. The part of the brain that adults rely on to regulate emotion and to problem-solve in stressful situations is not completely integrated until a person is roughly 24 to 30 years old. This part of the brain, called the prefrontal cortex, is essential for managing all emotions including anxiety and stress. As you can imagine, this makes it difficult for adolescents to understand and properly manage emotions like anxiety and stress. It's as if they are trying to complete a puzzle with several missing pieces or build a piece of furniture without a functioning hammer. Often, they do not have the proper materials to successfully manage anxiety and stress on their own.

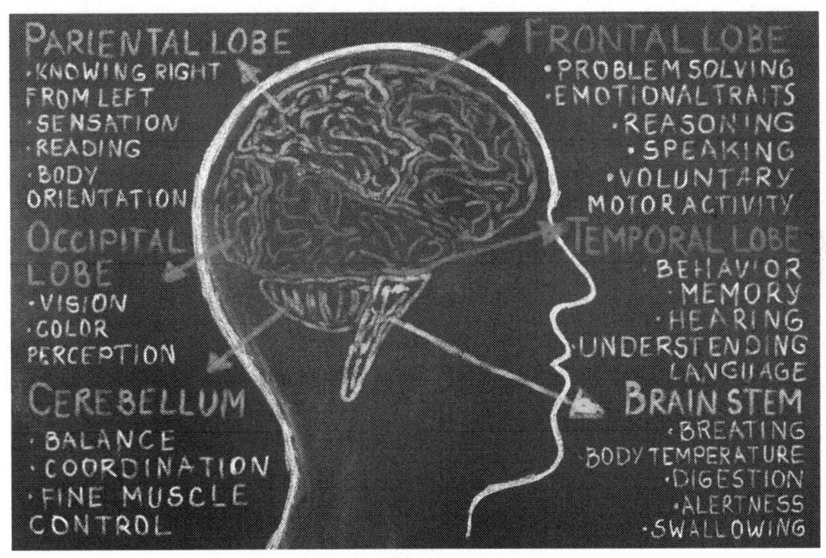

Figure 1
Human Brian Structure

IMAGE SOURCE: iStock (Standard License)

As we see in Figure 1, the different parts of the brain serve very different functions. As discussed in the preceding paragraph, the frontal lobe (or prefrontal cortex) is essential for adult-level decision-making, planning, and problem solving, for expressing emotional traits, and for reasoning, speaking, and voluntary motor activity. The "primal brain," as mentioned earlier in this chapter, includes the limbic structures that are located at the center of the brain beneath the cerebral cortex. The primal brain facilitates many non-conscious reactive systems such as the "fight or flight" mechanism. Can you imagine trying to manage your emotions without the full function of these very important parts of your brain?

With this background, we can see why adolescent brain development is the main factor in approaching anxiety management differently with young people compared with adults. For example, it is essential that young people have adults they trust who can help them understand their anxiety and to collaborate on ways to manage all that they are feeling. Ideally, they have a parent to support them in the process. However, even when a young person has a supportive parent, he or she will often seek out an adult other than a parent. Young people commonly turn to a youth pastor, coach, teacher or friend when they need help. This is a natural and healthy attempt to broaden their emotional support system and to individuate from their family system. A broader support system can also offer young people a sense of perspective, another component that is more difficult to acquire earlier in life.

Not only can anxiety and stress be more difficult to properly manage during adolescence and young adulthood, they can also be more difficult to identify, for a number of reasons. Young people are just getting to know themselves as people and as adult members of society, and might not have insight into their own feelings or moods. Their functioning can be quite dynamic. Later in this chapter, for example, we will discuss specific adolescent symptoms of anxiety and stress. As you look at the list of symptoms, you might say to yourself, “This is how I experience adolescents most of the time” (that is, unusual sleeping and eating patterns, difficulty focusing, moodiness, irritable, interpersonal problems, worry, etc.). Finally, adolescents also face the challenges of puberty and rapid hormonal development.

Simply put, it is crucial for adults to have conversations with struggling adolescents due to most younger persons’ general inability to fully recognize the nature and cause of the symptoms of anxiety. Additionally, discussing an adolescent’s internal world is extremely important in helping to identify and differentiate mental health issues (personal or relational) as opposed to the influence of normal adolescent hormonal changes.

The Types of Anxiety-Related Disorders

If a diagnosis is made, the following terms are often used:

Generalized Anxiety Disorder (GAD):

The person reports a sense of overwhelm and of excessive worry, with a constant expectation that something very bad will happen in the future to either themselves, school, family, friends or health. They cannot be calmed easily, if at all. This issue must persist for at least 6 months to be diagnosed as GAD.

> Although anxiety affects both females and males, females appear to develop anxiety disorders at a rate that is nearly double to that of males.

Panic disorder:

This disorder is diagnosed when a person has experienced multiple panic attacks over the period of at least one month, and they fear they will experience more. Typically, the panic attack will include a sudden and surprising feeling of intense terror that is not appropriate to the situation. The worry is so great that the body will react with a racing heart, shortness of breath, sweat, and/or dizziness. These are all symptoms similar to a heart attack, and sometimes the person fears she or he is dying or choking. A person can also have an isolated panic attack without it becoming a longer-lasting disorder.

Phobias:

This excessive fear of some tangible thing, or of a specific situation, can cause an individual to take great measures to avoid the feared scenario. A common phobia is agoraphobia, for example. The person may avoid certain situations such as public places or crowds in order to not be overwhelmed with anxiety or have a panic attack. Other specific phobias are triggered by bugs, snakes, flying, or what are normally considered difficult or unpleasant situations, like having blood drawn.

*(Note that not all people who faint when having blood drawn are fearful or phobic. Nurses and phlebotomists know this can also be an **involuntary** reaction, apart from an overall anxious state.)*

The Data

Among adults and adolescents, anxiety is the most common form of mental illness. Unfortunately, it is often not recognized as anxiety, and, therefore, not properly treated. Anxiety symptoms can include physical, psychological, social, and spiritual issues. An estimated 31.9% of adolescents in the U.S. will experience some form of anxiety disorder during their lifetime, with 8.3% experiencing severe impairment (NIMH, 2017).

In both adults and adolescents, females are diagnosed with anxiety disorders at a rate nearly double that of males. Although the causes for this disparity are not fully known, many have speculated that they may range from innate biological differences between adolescent males and females, to differences in their home life, socialization, and the multiple roles that young women may play (such as caregivers for younger siblings), to the possibility that males under-report their anxiety symptoms, and instead describe them in physiological terms (such as muscle tension or gastrointestinal complaints). Additionally, young men may be more likely than young women to channel their anxiety and stress into versions of anger, such as irritability and aggression. Young women, however, are generally socialized to not directly express their anger, which often mutates into anxiety, isolation, and withdrawal, resulting in a sort of "slow burn". Though neither of these patterns is universal, these less functional responses to stress and anxiety can cause confusion about the actual nature of the underlying problem, and can also exacerbate any existing relational tensions.

While nearly 32% of 13- to 18-year-olds experienced an anxiety disorder in the year prior to a recent study (NIMH, 2017), a significant increase has been projected to follow the current COVID-19 pandemic and general social unrest in the U.S. Additionally, it is estimated that as many as 75% of those who experience anxiety disorders are also experiencing symptoms of significant depression. Therefore, when you hear someone describing symptoms consistent with an anxiety disorder, you should *also* listen for signs of co-occurring depression and even suicidal thoughts (further described in our chapter on depression).

What are the Common Symptoms of Adolescent Anxiety and Stress?

Below are two lists of possible symptoms of both stress and anxiety. You will notice some overlap. Remember that, with stress, the symptoms will resolve once the precipitating stressor is removed. In contrast, anxiety may persist even after the stressor is removed. You will also notice, as mentioned earlier, that many of these symptoms can occur even in the absence of anxiety or stress, due to the impacts of development.

STRESS

The symptoms of stress may include:

Physical:
- Bodily pain, such as headaches *(also common with hormonal change)*
- Stomach problems
- Sleep disturbance and fatigue *(also common with hormonal changes)*

Psychological:
- Anxiety
- Problems with focus *(also common with hormonal change)*
- Feeling overwhelmed *(also common with hormonal change)*
- Irritability and anger *(also common with hormonal change)*
- Depression *(also common with hormonal change)*
- Addiction to food or substances
- Moodiness *(also common with hormonal change)*

Social:
- Withdrawal from others or activities once loved
- Avoidance
- Appearing distracted or preoccupied *(also common with hormonal change)*
- Shutting down to avoid feeling flooded or overwhelmed *(more likely without prefrontal cortex integration)*
- Interpersonal issues (parents, teachers, friends)

Spiritual:
- Life feels meaningless
- Lack of forgiveness
- Avoidance of God
- Guilty feelings *(also common with hormonal change)*
- Anger at God
- Doubt

ANXIETY

The symptoms of anxiety may include:

Physical:
- Heart beating fast, chest pains *(also common with hormonal change)*
- Feeling flushed *(also common with hormonal change)*
- Dizziness, headache *(also common with hormonal change)*
- Sweating *(also common with hormonal change)*
- Numbing
- Stomachache, nausea, diarrhea, throwing up *(also common with hormonal change)*
- Various muscle pains, constant tenseness *(also common with hormonal change)*
- Inability to sleep and constant tiredness *(also common with hormonal change)*
- Breathing: hyperventilation, feeling like you can't breathe

Psychological:
- Need for constant reassurance due to excessive worry
- Inability to perceive situations realistically *(more likely without prefrontal cortex integration)*
- Intrusive agitating thoughts *(more likely without prefrontal cortex integration)*
- Dissociation and numbing of feelings *(more likely without prefrontal cortex integration)*
- Excessive dependence
- Indecisiveness *(more likely without prefrontal cortex integration)*
- Disturbing dreams *(also common with hormonal change)*
- Irritability *(also common with hormonal change)*
- Development of phobias
- Obsessive thoughts and compulsive behaviors

Social:
- Avoiding relationships or situations that are perceived to produce more anxiety
- Using relationships for relief, more so than for connection or ongoing intimacy
- Overwhelming fear of embarrassing oneself
- Difficulty meeting new people
- Isolating

Spiritual:
- Lack of enjoyment of God
- Seeing anxiety as a sin with ensuing feelings of guilt and badness
- Feelings of insecurity relative to God
- Questioning whole belief system *(also common with adolescent development)*

These are general symptom patterns, and some young people might experience symptoms from both lists. For example, an anxious person can experience stress, and a stressed person can develop anxiety after a period of strain (for example, becoming "distressed", or experiencing post-traumatic stress disorder, or "PTSD").

Common Causes of Stress or Anxiety

Those in our faith communities will likely express concerns without attaching specific labels to their experiences. As with stress and anxiety symptoms, the causes or concerns can also be grouped into two broad categories.

Stress can be triggered by:

- School, sports or work challenges
- Learning issues, bullying, grades, and feeling overscheduled
- Friendships/romantic relationships
- Family issues - divorce, neglect or over-parenting, sibling rivalry, etc.
- Significant life changes - new school, moving into a new home, parents' divorce, etc.
- Chronic illness
- Technology
- Social media
- Societal changes
- Family financial problems
- Grief and loss

Anxiety can be triggered by:

- School and grades
- Friendships
- Unresolved early trauma
- Feelings of abandonment (family/ friends)
- Temperament and personality disposition
- Gender-related demands and strain
- Race or ethnicity related demands and tension
- Genetic predisposition
- Medical conditions, such as hyperthyroidism and Vitamin B12 deficiency
- Technology including social media
- Substance abuse and withdrawal
- Traumatic, compound, or complicated losses and grief
- Concerns about Sexual identity

Working in ministry, we might not be aware of all of the causes and symptoms listed here. So what are the ***most likely*** red flags for stress?

- Sleep disturbance *(also common with hormonal changes)*
- Eating disturbance *(also common with hormonal changes)*
- Irritability *(also common with hormonal changes)*
- Withdrawal/isolation from friends and/or support system
- Severe physical complaints
- Change in grades

IMAGE SOURCE: Pixabay

And the ***most likely*** red flags for anxiety are:

- Needing constant reassurance in the midst of excessive worry about anything
- Inability to complete schoolwork or having distress in relationships
- Complaints of physical pain due to worry
- Focus on fear of the future and excessive concerns of something negative happening
- Avoids leaving the house and does not want to go to school
- No longer involved in activities they once loved- sports, school clubs, youth group, etc.

Risk Factors for Developing an Anxiety Disorder

Although it is often difficult to determine the specific cause of an anxiety disorder, experts have narrowed down some likely factors. Many are related to the biopsychosocialspiritual model described earlier in this manual. As one can imagine, genetic and biological predispositions have been implicated, based on studies of symptoms among relatives. Psychological factors such as parental and family dynamics, personal losses, and a tendency to catastrophize difficult situations are also common among those with anxiety disorders.

Often those who struggle with anxiety and severe stress have difficulty maintaining stability and connections to social and familial relationships, because the internal experience of anxiety is a battle that can result in either withdrawal from or excessive need for such connections. Either of these tendencies are disruptive to important relationships. In addition, one's relationship with God can also be disrupted by anxiety and stress. Feelings of being "spiritually weak" or "not trusting God enough" are often described by anxious Christians. These judgements, by themselves or others, can result in a conflicted set of feelings toward God and as well as distorted beliefs about how God experiences and cares for them.

The 4 D's of Mental Illness

Let's summarize the information in this chapter using the 4 D's.

Deviance—How might a young person's symptoms differ from what one would normally expect to see under similar circumstances?

____

____

Dysfunction—How might a person's experience of the disorder(s) potentially interfere with their ability to function in day-to-day life (e.g., school, relationship, etc.)?

____

____

Distress—Describe the biopsychosocialspiritual distress that might be associated with the disorder(s).

____

____

Danger —What types of words or actions might suggest that the person you're interacting with is in some type of danger?

____

____

LASER

Now, use the LASER to evaluate the experiences and possible responses suggesting a more serious mental health concern.

LISTEN for key words that suggest someone may be struggling with a mental health condition

ASSESS the type and severity of the mental health issue presented

STRATEGIZE to develop a potential response to the mental health concern

EXPLORE potential interventions with the afflicted individual as well as the accessibility and openness to these options

REFER to appropriate mental health professionals when necessary

LISTEN

LISTEN for key words that suggest someone may be struggling with a mental health condition

- I worry all of the time... about a lot of different things.
- My friends or parents tell me that I'm often quite irritable or easily angered.
- I often feel overwhelmed by my life.
- I drink or use prescription or non-prescription drugs to manage my fears and worries.
- I tend to avoid people because it just feels overwhelming to deal with all of their issues.
- I carry a lot of tension in my shoulders and back.
- I have a lot of gastrointestinal problems that are unexplained.
- Life feels so overwhelming that I sometimes think about hurting myself.
- I feel bad when I think about God.
- I feel like my worry must disappoint God.

NOTES:

ASSESS the type and severity of the mental health issue presented

ASSESS

- Determine if the concern is situational stress or problematic anxiety.
- Have they experienced a panic attack or fear they will?
- Is their anxiety creating significant disruption in the family, at school or with friends?
- How long have they been carrying this level of anxiety?
- Are they experiencing physical symptoms such as frequent muscle tension or stomach aches?
- Are they struggling to use their normal coping skills and supports to manage their anxiety?

NOTES:

STRATEGIZE

STRATEGIZE to develop a potential response to the mental health concern

- Collaborate and brainstorm options the young person has considered in the past, which were either helpful or unhelpful, and why.
- Has the person had a recent medical exam and/or an evaluation for medication?
- What is the role of technology and social media in this person's life?
- Has the young person's thyroid levels been recently checked?
- What type of life circumstances could they cut-out or minimize to decrease anxiety or stress?
- Explore possible mindfulness apps such as *Headspace* and/or *Calm* to help manage symptoms (e.g., mindfulness teaches physical and emotional awareness and allows for more adaptive reactions to difficult situation).
- Do they have a consistent person they can meet with regularly who can care for them in their stress or anxiety? This person could be a therapist, pastor, grandparent or friend who is available to them.
- Have they been able to stay connected, or have relationships been strained?

NOTES:

EXPLORE potential interventions with the afflicted individual as well as the accessibility and openness to these options

EXPLORE

- Therapy may be helpful in identifying coping strategies and helpful interventions.
- Exercise is a helpful intervention for anxiety and depression. Taking into account any medical advice or health-related barriers, how can one integrate exercise into daily life?
- Help set up some type of accountability to taking first steps to address the issues.
- Ask questions to see how open the person is to the potential strategies discussed above.
- Help them set up a mindfulness app on a cell phone.
- Discuss potential care ministries within their church community (for example, youth group; small groups oriented toward mental health; DivorceCare for Kids).
- Work with the person to create or to share an existing list of community resources they might be open to exploring. (If no list is available, contact United Way 2-1-1 online.)

NOTES:

REFER

REFER to appropriate mental health professionals when necessary

- Anxiety and stress disorders are highly treatable, if the individual is willing and able to follow through.
- A psychologist (Ph.D. or Psy.D.), social worker (MSW or LCSW), or marriage and family therapist (MFT) would be an appropriate referral for someone suffering with anxiety and stress.
- The therapist may refer the person to a physician for a general medical evaluation.
- The therapist may also refer the person to a psychiatrist to see if medications might be a reasonable aspect of treatment.
- Seeking spiritual direction in addition to therapy may be helpful in addressing the young person's experience of God during this time, provided that the symptoms of anxiety are sufficiently managed.

NOTES:

Important Take-Aways for Ministry Leaders

- We all experience stress and anxiety to varying degrees, because it is a part of our basic biological survival system.
- Adolescents and young adults experience and process anxiety and stress differently from adults, especially due to differences in brain and physical development.
- Youth pastors and ministry leaders can contribute significantly to the emotional well-being and management of stress and anxiety among adolescents and young adults.
- The primary difference between anxiety and stress is that stress comes from some external demand or factor that often can be addressed and resolved.
- Anxiety is the internal state, or a way that we cope with stress.
- Many aspects of stress can be reduced and managed by getting adequate sleep, exercise, nutrition and hydration.
- Anxiety is the most common mental illness you will encounter, impacting as many as 32% of adolescents.
- As many as 75% of those who experience anxiety disorders are also experiencing symptoms of significant depression.

RESOURCES

Online Organizations and Support:

Anxiety Disorder Association of America (child and teens): www.adaa.org

Anxiety Panic Attack Resource Site: www.anxietypanic.com

Fuller Youth Institute: fulleryouthinstitute.org

National Alliance on Mental Illness (NAMI): https://www.nami.org/

United Way 211: A virtual service to connect individuals to support https://www.211unitedway.org

Videos:

Anxiety: 11 Things We Want You to Understand (available on You Tube)

Jonas Kolker, ***Tedx The Masters School: Overcoming Anxiety*** https://www.youtube.com/watch?v=A1anXJhVamc

UCLA Mindfulness Lab: https://www.uclahealth.org/marc/

Books:

Siegel, Daniel J. (2015). ***Brainstorm: The power and purpose of the teenage brain.*** New York , NY: Penguin. ISBN-10: 158542935X

Willard, Christopher (2014). ***Mindfulness for teen anxiety.*** Oakland, CA: New Harbinger Publications.

Apps:

(Note: These are examples, not endorsements by the author.)

Calm

One-Minute Meditation (OMM)

Headspace

Self-help for Anxiety Management (SAM)

UCLA Mindful App

REFERENCES

National Institute for Mental Health (2017). ***Any anxiety disorder.*** Retrieved from https://www.nimh.nih.gov/health/statistics/any-anxiety-disorder.shtml

IMAGE SOURCE: Shutterstock (Standard License)

"Yet there is one ray of hope: his compassion never ends. It is only the Lord's mercies that have kept us from complete destruction. Great is his faithfulness; his loving-kindness begins afresh each day"

— Lamentations 3:21-23

Holly Morris, LMFT
Laura Wingard, MA, LMFT

Adolescent Trauma and Post-Traumatic Stress Disorder (PTSD)

The Nature of Trauma

In our current culture, the word "***trauma***" and the acronym "***PTSD***" (referring to ***post-traumatic stress disorder***) have become commonplace. When these terms are used casually, people are often referring to an experience that evoked shock and fear, followed by a stress reaction at the reminder of that experience. Four out of five people diagnosed with post-traumatic stress disorder (PTSD) are also diagnosed with at least one other mental health condition (American Psychiatric Association, 2013). Therefore, many mental health struggles have a trauma component.

What is helpful about trauma language becoming more mainstream is that may evoke curiosity to understand what trauma is, as well as how people experience and heal from it. However, there may also be a risk of missing the nuanced severity of traumatic impact. The goal of this chapter is to create a trauma-informed lens through which to compassionately consider the nature of traumatic experiences and the impact they can have on the lives of adolescents.

For most people, post-traumatic stress (PTS) will begin to decrease and subside within the first several weeks after a trauma. Involvement in life responsibilities, relationships and interests return to levels prior to the incident. For others, the psychological and biological systems—key components of our biopsychosocialspiritual model—have difficulty returning to a normal state of equilibrium; in that case, the symptoms may increase in severity, resulting in a diagnosis of PTSD. Therefore, a broadening or an increase in symptoms helps indicate when it would be beneficial to refer to a mental health professional.

Trauma disrupts a young person's life in a manner that may decrease the sense of personal safety in the world. For some young people, internal resources may be limited simply based on age and experience. The task of a young person in resolving trauma can be further complicated by lack of neurological resources. Developmentally, they simply have less experience with healthy emotional coping and with healthy trauma resolution than adults. A young person's brain is still developing and not yet fully capable of emotional regulation, of predicting consequences, or of having access to proper judgement in many novel situations. Resources may also be external, such as monetary, legal, relational support and provision of basic needs. When resources are lacking and the impact of an event is significant, the risk of severity of trauma increases. Conversely, sufficient resources support a decrease in intensity and duration of PTS.

While trauma may be a one-time incident or a series of compounding incidents, there is a common outcome: the individual who has experienced the stress has been changed. This change may create a need for the traumatized person to process the impact, in order to make sense of the experience in the context of his or her life and to regain a sense of safety in the world in mind, body and spirit. The sooner someone begins to process the trauma, the sooner symptoms begin to decrease. Treatment, in most cases, will also help to prevent or to slow the development of other potentially debilitating symptoms.

As a ministry leader or educator, it is important to be familiar with the symptoms of PTS and PTSD, in order to help normalize the initial responses to crisis as well as to monitor any increase in severity. It is also important to be aware of any triggers that you might personally carry, and to take steps to address them even as you support others.

The Data

Prevalence

While an estimated 50% to 89% of all people will experience a crisis in their lifetimes (Owens, 2016), a much smaller percentage will develop diagnosable PTSD. Looking at Figure 1, the data show that an estimated 5% of adolescents show lifetime prevalence of PTSD, while 1.5% will have severe impairment. According to the according to this National Comorbidity Survey study, the prevalence of PTSD among adolescents was higher for females (8.0%) than for males (2.3%).

Lifetime Prevalence of Post-Traumatic Stress disorder Among Adolescents (2001-2004)

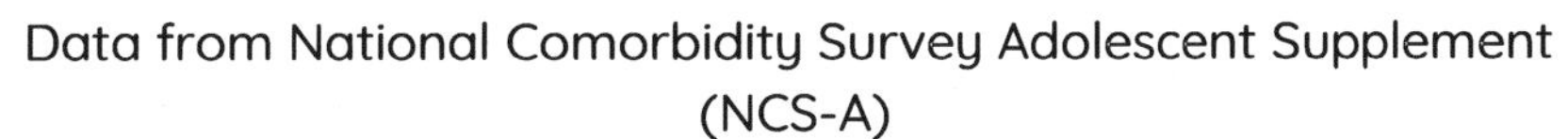

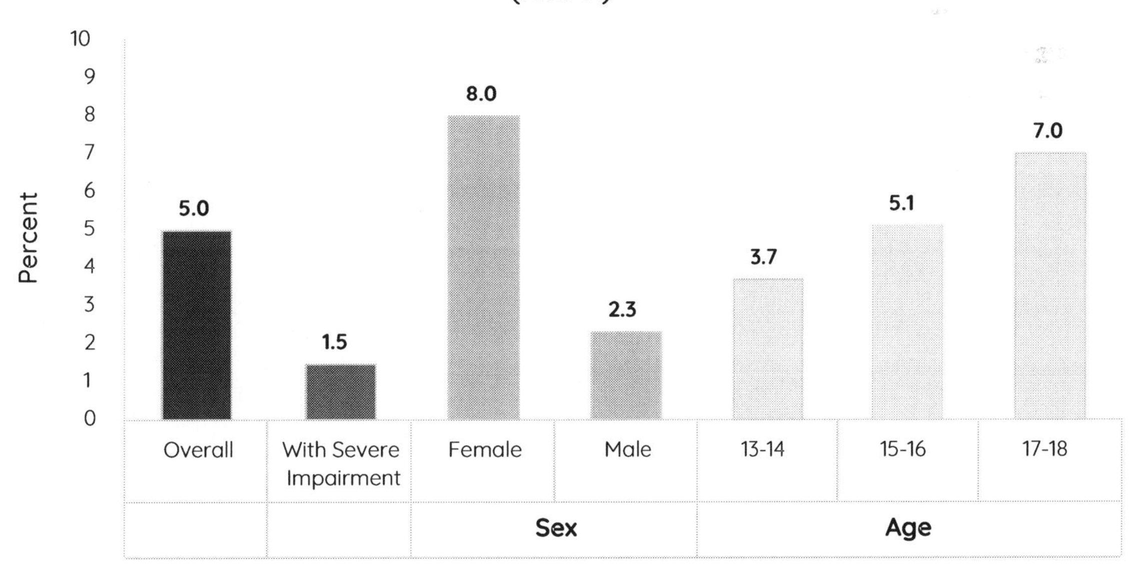

Figure 1

Prevalence of PTSD among adolescents, NIH data

SOURCE: https://www.nimh.nih.gov/health/statistics/post-traumatic-stress-disorder-ptsd.shtml

Health Impact of Trauma

While most people have experienced a traumatic event in their lifetimes, the impact varies. One helpful approach to conceptualizing the potential severity of traumatic events on an individual is to consider the risk factors from early development. An informative study of more than 17,000 adults was conducted from 1995 to 1997 with patients at Kaiser Permanente in Southern California. This study confidentially surveyed adults who had reported on adverse life events at between 0 and 17 years of age, using 10 questions about Adverse Childhood Experiences (ACEs). These experiences were defined as child abuse, child neglect and household events that challenged the safety, security, and stability of household members. The purpose of the study was to discover if there was a positive correlation between ACEs and negative health conditions.

The results of this study indicated that:

- 65% of respondents reported one or more ACEs
- Nearly 15% reported four or more ACEs
- Correlations *were* found between the reported ACEs and detrimental health conditions

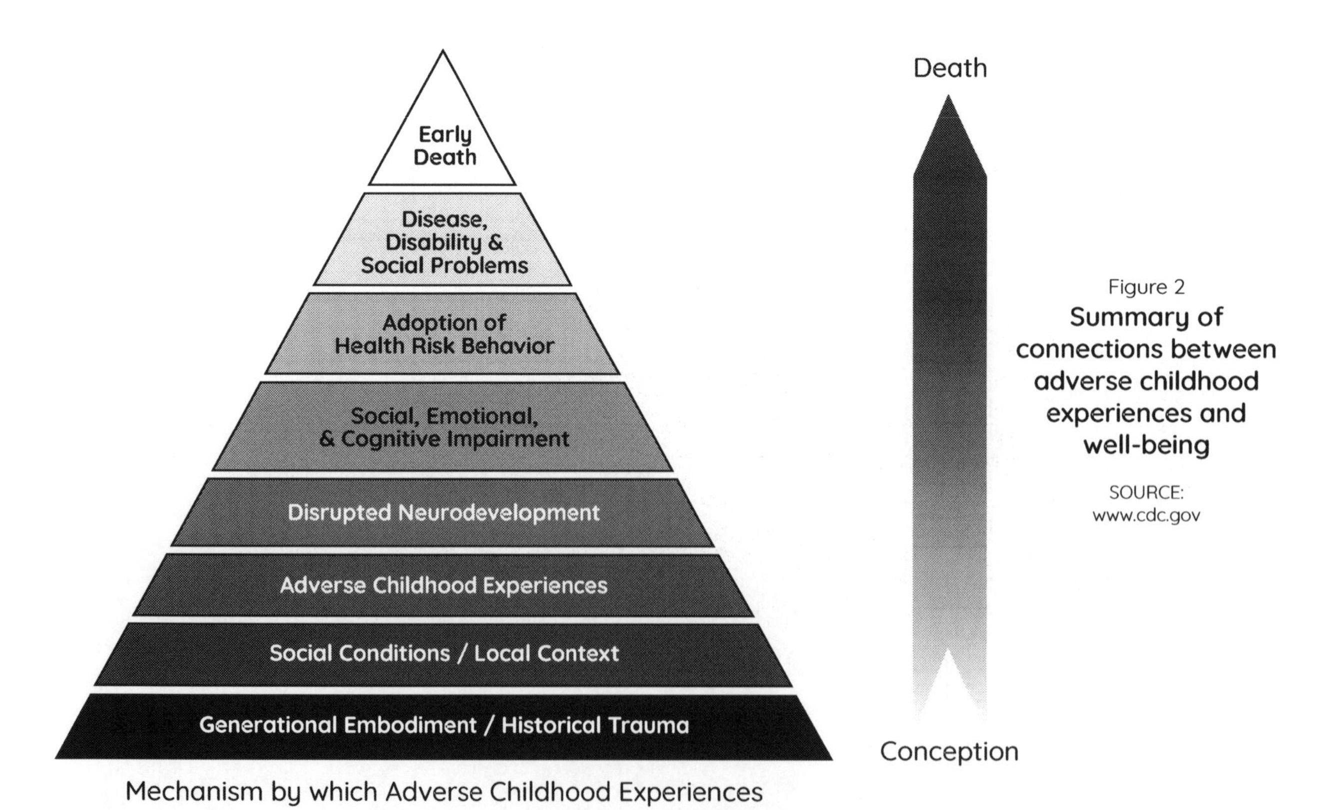

Mechanism by which Adverse Childhood Experiences Influence Health and Well-being Throughout the Lifespan

Figure 2
Summary of connections between adverse childhood experiences and well-being

SOURCE: www.cdc.gov

The layered and compounded impact of ACEs on the development of individuals and their overall well-being throughout their lifetimes is depicted in the image of the ACEs pyramid in Figure 2. The ACEs questionnaire continues to be utilized to gain information for further research and as an assessment tool to create plans for prevention and intervention. When specifically considering the impact of a "big T" trauma, persons with higher ACEs scores would be more likely to develop symptoms of PTSD than those with lower to zero ACEs.

Trauma's Impact on the Body

As the foundational layers indicate, a lack of security in relationships, defined by too much adversity and/or too little nurturing, safety or security may result in toxic stress, leading to an impact that can be life-long. In physical terms, toxic stress is caused by the survival stress response activation and the release of stress hormones with a high frequency and for a long duration of time. The research suggests the toxic stress response affects:

- **Physiology:** Underdevelopment in brain regions that promote emotional regulation, problem-solving, ability to focus, retention of information
- **Behavior:** smoking, over-eating, high number of sexual partners, substance abuse
- **Mental health:** depression, anxiety, suicide
- **Physical health:** asthma, heart disease, obesity, sexually transmitted diseases, chronic pain, autoimmune disorders
- **Early death**

The intricate and complex design of the human body includes a hard-wired, biological system organized to survive. When a young person experiences a traumatic event, specific regions of their brain automatically direct the nervous system to activate a *fight, flight* or *freeze* response in the body. The sympathetic nervous system then activates or intensifies certain body processes (such as heart rate, muscle tension, blood pressure, dilated pupils, increased stress hormones) in preparation to fight or flee. Conversely, the parasympathetic nervous system is utilized to down-shift or reduce the same functions in order to avoid further injury or death.

While the fight/flight/freeze (FFF) response is helpful at the time of incident, problems occur when the body becomes stuck in that state for too long, including reported impacts to health and general functioning.

Categories of Trauma

In the mental health world, trauma is described in three categories: "big T" trauma, "little t" trauma and cumulative trauma. "Big T" traumas may be caused by humans, such as an incident of abuse, sexual or physical violence, or a car accident, or they may be outside human control, such as a natural disaster, a death, an earthquake, a tsunami or a fire. "Big T" trauma events are often sudden experiences that create a significant, immediate impact on a person. In the longer term, "big T" trauma disrupts someone's world and may even change it.

"Little t" trauma describes experiences that were impactful due to the context or to the young person's developmental stage. Often tied to humiliation or abandonment, the events may not be as obvious in their personal impact, yet they were defining for the individual (Shapiro, 2001) . "Little t" trauma may create a vulnerability to be negatively impacted by future trauma.

Cumulative trauma has a layered impact and includes individual and/or collective traumatic experiences, chronic experiences of the same trauma, or the compounded impact of several types of trauma. Collective trauma can involve a system as intimate as a family or as broad as an entire social group. Examples include witnessing domestic violence or child abuse, or consistent exposure to war or military occupation, crime, racism and actions based on prejudice and poverty. The complexity of the impact of cumulative trauma affects a person's view of themselves, others, God and the world around them, affecting self-image and the general sense of safety in the world.

IMAGE SOURCE: Pixabay

Specific Aspects of Trauma

Four markers define when a crisis event may be traumatic enough to cause lingering, potentially life-altering impacts. Crisis events may become traumatic when they include:

1. **A real or perceived threat of being in danger** of death, serious injury or sexual violence. This includes events directly experienced by an individual, or as witnessed or experienced as a third-party through story-telling. Repetitive exposure to traumatic events at work also applies.
2. **The event causes a significant loss** of something, such as a person, property, personal status/reputation or sense of perceived safety in the world.
3. **A real or perceived sense the situation was inescapable.**
4. **Pre-existing vulnerability** to the traumatic impact due to previous negative life experiences, current resource deficits and current life-stressors.

It may be tempting to evaluate and/or anticipate the impact of a crisis situation by the *appearance* of severity of the event. As an example, an accident resulting in a car fire may appear to be more traumatic than an accident with much less damage. What is reflected in the research supports the traumatic impact being individualistic in nature, affected by a variety of details specific to each situation. The most important way for those in ministry to understand the traumatic impact a person is experiencing is by being a caring presence and asking thoughtful questions.

TIPS FOR TAMING TRAUMA

While those in ministry should not attempt to provide therapy, these are some helpful ways that young people can use to help regulate their own FFF responses.

- 10 deep breaths (in through nose, out through mouth)
- 15 jumping jacks
- Reading aloud
- Taking a cold shower
- Taking a short, brisk walk
- Using anchoring phrases such as: "My name is______, and I'm ____ years old. I live in the city of ______, and in the state of______. Today is ______. It's 10:04 in the morning. I'm sitting at my desk at school. There's no one else in the room. I am safe."
- Using the Safe Place Technique (imagine a place you feel comfort or safe)
- Describing aloud what the person sees in his or her environment
- Petting a cat or dog

What are the Common Symptoms of Adolescent Trauma and Post-Traumatic Stress?

As PTS is experienced over time without intervention, symptoms typically intensify and become compounded. Also, as the severity of symptoms increases, there is a broadening of impact on the person's life and a negative impact on sense of self-worth. Symptoms may include:

Physical

- Hypervigilance
- Exaggerated startle response
- Rapid heartbeat
- Breathing problems
- Tight muscles
- Sleep problems: Sleeping too much, Difficulty falling asleep or staying asleep, Nightmares
- Difficulty with concentration and memory retention
- Blanking out mentally/losing track of time
- Numbing out
- Physical pain
- Chronic fatigue
- Immune system problems
- Issues with maintaining healthy body weight
- Illnesses without medical explanation: chronic headaches, digestion issues

Psychological

- Fear
- Grief
- Guilt
- Anxiety
- Frequent crying
- Hyperactivity
- Denial
- Avoidance
- Rage
- Poor decisions
- Abrupt, minimized or exaggerated emotional responses
- Paranoia
- Depression
- Forgetfulness
- Dissociation
- Shame
- Apathy
- Suicidal/homicidal

Social

- Irritability
- Lack of enjoyment in social activities
- Lack of interest in connecting with others
- Fear of trusting others
- Overly dependent
- Isolation
- Missing commitments: work, school, social engagements, responsibilities
- Inability to nurture or bond with other individuals
- Acting out in anger toward others
- Excessive shyness
- Fear of rejection and abandonment
- Exaggerated or diminished sexual activity
- Feelings of detachment, isolation

Spiritual

- Hopelessness
- Questioning God's goodness
- Uncertainty about God's provision/ protection
- Loss of faith
- Increase in faith
- Guilt
- Difficulty trusting others or trusting too freely
- Comparison of faith experiences
- Feeling unlovable/unworthy of God
- Difficulty attaching to God and faith community

According to National Institute of Mental Health (NIMH), young people can have extreme reactions to trauma, but their symptoms may not always be identical to those in adults. Young people may also become overly clingy with friends or family, or may develop disruptive, disrespectful or destructive behaviors. They may also feel guilty for not preventing the traumatic events or experience thoughts of revenge.

Diagnostic Categories

To provide effective treatment, five categories of PTS symptoms are assessed for diagnosis and severity, per the *Diagnostic and Statistical Manual of Mental Disorders (5th ed.) (DSM-5):*

- **Intrusion**: spontaneous thoughts, dreams, memories of the traumatic event
- **Avoidance**: attempts to evade internal and external reminders of the event
- **Dissociation**: disconnection from the present moment, feeling "checked out" and often being checked in to another time or space internally
- **Negative Mood:** lack of feeling positive emotional states
- **Arousal:** restlessness in the form of agitation, startle response, lack of focus, aggression, disruption in sleep patterns

The resulting sub-categories of the diagnosis can then be made, including:

Acute Stress Disorder (ASD): This person has experienced a traumatic event which has been followed by several of the symptoms from the categories listed above. These symptoms have impacted their ability to maintain their lifestyle to include work, relationships, responsibilities and pleasurable activities to the same capacity as prior to the event. A person may be diagnosed with ASD for up to 30 days after the traumatic event.

Post-Traumatic Stress Disorder (PTSD): This person has experienced a traumatic event and is displaying a severity of PTS symptoms in number of categories and/or intensity of symptoms for 30 days or longer. Symptoms often include a drive to avoid any remembrance of the event resulting in a narrowing of life involvements and overall life satisfaction. In some circumstances there may be delayed onset of PTSD, such as when a current life event activates PTS symptoms from a traumatic event that occurred earlier in life.

Complex Trauma/Complex PTSD (C-PTSD): This is not a diagnosis included in the DSM-5, but it is widely recognized and utilized by mental health professionals. Someone with Complex Trauma or Complex PTSD has experienced trauma during his or her developmental years, in a systemic or chronical nature, such as not receiving enough security or nurturing. This is trauma is often combined with too much negative attention through abuse. Due to the nature of repetition and timing of the incidents, this type of trauma has a negative impact on a person's self-perception, satisfaction in relationship with others, ability to regulate emotions and connect meaningfully with themselves, others and God.

Long-Term Triggers for Traumatic Memories

During the activation of the FFF response, the internal experience and the external environment are remembered or stored by the brain *and* the body. These data points of memory are stored in the brain through sensory inputs, such as sight, sound, smell, touch and taste. Here is an example of what may develop from an auto accident:

- **Sight:** bright lights, colors of anything involved, people
- **Sound:** loud bang, breaking glass, honking horns, screaming
- **Smell:** smoke, gasoline, burned tires, hot brakes
- **Tactile:** pain in any area of body impacted or that made contact with the automobile or other persons or objects
- **Taste:** anything in the mouth at time of incident, including blood, if injured

When a person has contact with those specific sensory data points, often referred to as a "trigger", the brain responds as if exposed to the *original* traumatic threat, and it activates the nervous system in a similar manner. Over time, the triggers may activate FFF in settings without any obvious connection to the original trauma. From the example above, the loud bang of a firework or the smell of gasoline at a gas pump may activate the FFF. *The avoidance of re-experiencing these symptoms becomes the keystone of PTS.* Therefore, without intervention, a traumatized person's world is at risk of becoming smaller and less satisfying in all areas of life as he or she seeks to avoid triggers.

Providing a basic understanding of the FFF survival system can be empowering for persons affected by trauma. It contains knowledge to challenge a common belief that they were "weak" or are "going crazy". Reinforcing the fact that an apparent overreaction or underreaction of the body in order to survive may be a powerful support and comfort, softening guilt and shame.

Treatment

Early intervention is best. When someone you are ministering to or a friend or family member is experiencing mild to severe PTS, it can be confusing and sometimes frightening. Their experiences may be uncomfortable to hear, and it may be heartbreaking and frustrating to see someone you care about suffering in ways that are changing them. You may notice changes in personality, mood, activity and demeanor that lead to further isolation within the relationship. These changes are warning signs to find professional help.

As trauma impacts the biopsychosocialspiritual aspects of a person, therapeutic treatment addresses each of these aspects. Treatment often includes:

- Education about how trauma impacts the system of a person
- Teaching strategies for relaxation and stress reduction
- Creating language for the person to share their experience
- Processing through difficult beliefs, shame, fear
- Discovering meaning in the experience

One important aspect of the healing journey is the uncovering and enhancing of personal resiliency. In this context, ***resiliency*** can be defined as the ability to navigate successfully and to brave life's challenges as they arise. As resiliency is embodied, often there are spontaneous discoveries of hope, gratitude, connection or reward, often referred to as post-traumatic growth. Some passionate advocates for the help, healing and justice of others have been motivated by post-traumatic growth. This is a way, in the right and natural time, beauty may be born out of the ash of trauma.

Mandatory Reporting

It is common for young people who have experienced abuse to develop some form of traumatic response. While it is extremely heartbreaking to learn that a young person has been abused, this is also an opportunity to advocate and to help begin the process of healing through early intervention. Particularly for younger children, expressions or symptoms of difficulty can occur without the minor being able to recall details of the abuse. In addition, especially with chronic emotional abuse or neglect, these details may even appear "normal" to the minor.

When a minor (anyone under the age of 18) reports an incident, or when those in ministry "reasonably suspect" that a minor has been abused, those adults should make a report to Child Protective Services (CPS). Because pastors and educators are considered mandated reporters in most states, they must:

- Report abuse immediately to CPS via telephone, then follow up in writing
- Complete forms as instructed by CPS
- Mandatory reporters must provide their names; volunteer ministry workers may make anonymous reports

IMAGE SOURCE: Unsplash

After the report is completed, ministers have no further legal obligations. CPS or other trained professionals will develop a plan for continued care for the young person, as needed.

Ideally, the minor will be present for the call to CPS; however, in any case, there are legal consequences for *not* reporting suspected abuse to CPS. To become more confident in fulfilling their legal responsibilities, it's important for mandatory reports to be familiar with the nature of abuse. Ministers are encouraged to review the requirements in their states. The California Department of Education and the California Department of Social Services websites are provided at the end of this chapter.

Care for the Caregiver

IMAGE SOURCE: Unsplash

Because ministers provide interpersonal care, it is important that they receive support as well. If you find yourself feeling guilt, decreased empathy, increased stress, heightened irritability or other symptoms of PTS when caring for someone else, you may be experiencing ***vicarious trauma***. If so, it is especially important for you get proper rest, to continue to care for yourself and to seek support. Additionally, if the traumatized person is behaving in ways that put you in danger or at risk for injury, it is also critically important that you seek safety for yourself and all involved.

The 4 D's of Mental Illness

Let's summarize the information in this chapter using the 4 D's.

Deviance—How might a young person's symptoms differ from what one would normally expect to see under similar circumstances?

____

____

Dysfunction—How might a young person's experience of the disorder(s) potentially interfere with their ability to function in day-to-day life (for example, school, sports, relationship, etc.)?

____

____

Distress—Describe the biopsychosocialspiritual distress that might be associated with the disorder(s).

____

____

Danger —What types of words or actions might suggest that the young person you're interacting with is in some type of danger?

____

____

LASER

Now, use the LASER to evaluate the experiences and possible responses suggesting a more serious mental health concern.

for key words that suggest someone may be struggling with a mental health condition

ASSESS

the type and severity of the mental health issue presented

STRATEGIZE

to develop a potential response to the mental health concern

EXPLORE

potential interventions with the afflicted individual as well as the accessibility and openness to these options

REFER

to appropriate mental health professionals when necessary

LISTEN

LISTEN for key words that suggest someone may be struggling with a mental health condition

Since I had or have remembered a traumatic experience(s)...

- I cannot stop thinking about it.
- I have had difficulty sleeping.
- I am more irritable and/or easily angered.
- Memories of it come up in my mind, even for no reason.
- I have been feeling more anxious than usual.
- I get blank in my mind and time goes by without me noticing.
- I have started to or engaged in the use of substances with increased amount and/or time.
- I feel numb.
- I have felt scared to do things I used to enjoy.
- I have been missing school, social or extracurricular activities.
- I have been feeling detached from my life.
- Sometimes I think about killing or harming myself.
- I wonder if God loves me.
- I wonder if God is able/willing to protect me.
- I am afraid no one will understand me.
- I think I may be going crazy.

NOTES:

ASSESS the type and severity of the mental health issue presented

ASSESS

- How long ago did this event occur?
- What life circumstances have been impacted by this event?
- What are the symptoms of PTS the person is reporting?
- How have these symptoms impacted this person's ability to engage in their life activities of school, relationships, hobbies, etc.?
- Have others commented to the person about any changes they have witnessed?
- Does anyone outside of this person know the event occurred?
- How has this person been taking care of themselves? Seeking support?

NOTES:

STRATEGIZE

STRATEGIZE to develop a potential response to the mental health concern

- Familiarize yourself with the symptoms of PTS to communicate to the person, explain that what they are experiencing is expected, and help them to not feel crazy and/or isolated.
- Plan for a conversation with this person when there will be uninterrupted time.
- If meeting in person, make sure the person has access to a way out of the space without obstruction, in case they have any triggered fears about being trapped and need to escape.
- Does this person have a support network equipped to provide the particular support this person needs to heal?
- Gather resources to support any specific needs, tangible and mental-health-related in advance.
- Explore smart phone apps to help the person to identify feeling states and techniques to regulate symptoms.
- Keep in mind that early interventions of support are imperative to decreasing PTS symptoms and minimizing compounded impact to overall lifestyle/livelihood.

NOTES:

EXPLORE potential interventions with the afflicted individual as well as the accessibility and openness to these options

EXPLORE

- Listen generously to the person to determine their ability to engage in strategizing for next steps.
- Inquire about what they have done since noticing their life became altered (keep in mind a conversation with you may be their first step).
- Affirm the person for disclosing their experience and struggle; this is important as isolation and feeling "unrelatable" or "crazy" is common when someone is traumatized.
- Discuss the particulars of the person's support network and if there may be a trusted person to share their struggle.
- Discover any activities that have been avoided and may be tolerable to do again.
- Discuss what type of resources they may be willing to pursue: online community, in person community or ministry group, individual or group therapy, therapy by video platform from the setting of their choosing.
- Collaborate to create a plan for what resources they will explore and how/ when you can help and follow up with them.

NOTES:

REFER

REFER to appropriate mental health professionals when necessary

- Early intervention is an important part of someone's healing from experiencing trauma.
- As most people with PTSD are also experiencing other mental health issues, referrals to multiple resources may be helpful.
- A referral to a therapist who specializes in treating PTSD/C-PTSD is important, therefore have contact information available.
- Therapeutic treatments that focus on assisting the brain and body in processing the trauma have high success rates (for example, eye movement desensitization and reprocessing [EMDR]).
- Support ministries within the church, such as Celebrate Recovery, which may provide a place to process and connect someone as a bridge from isolation.

NOTES:

Important Take-Aways for Ministry Leaders

- Trauma is a human experience and affects many young people from mild to severe degrees.
- Knowledge and understanding about trauma can create a trauma-informed lens to evoke curiosity about the thoughts, behaviors and emotions of someone who has experienced trauma with compassion and empathy.
- Trauma can be caused when a person or someone they love has experienced a dangerous event that caused a significant loss and that felt inescapable.
- People are more susceptible to traumatization when they have had earlier trauma and/or have current life stressors.
- Trauma is an experience in the body followed by efforts to avoid re-experiencing the event or any reminders the event occurred.
- The God-designed biological survival system of fight/flight/freeze, which is facilitative at the time of incident, may create further injury if over-utilized.
- While PTSD and C-PTSD have some similarities, C-PTSD most negatively impacts a person's self-concept and creates challenge in trusting others and God.
- When a young person's life has been impacted by trauma, early intervention promotes best possibilities for adaptive resolution and return to pre-trauma functioning or beyond.

RESOURCES

Online Organizations and Support:

ACEs Connection: acesconnection.com

The Allender Center: theallendercenter.org

California Department of Education: https://www.cde.ca.gov/ls/ss/ap/childabusereportingguide.asp

California Department of Social Services: https://www.cdss.ca.gov/reporting/report-abuse

Gift From Within: giftfromwithin.org

My PTSD: myptsd.com

Nation Center for PTSD: ptsd.va.gov

Trauma Resource Institute: traumaresourceinstitute.com

Videos:

EMDR: https://youtube/hDivEv1U3Pg (documentary)

How childhood trauma affects health across a lifetime. Nadine Burke Harris, TEDMED: https://youtu.be/95ovIJ3dsNk

Understanding PTSD's effects on brain, body, and emotions. Janet Seahorn, TEDxCSU: https://www.youtube.com/watch?v=BEHDQeIRTgs&t=5s

Books:

Miller-Karas, Elaine (2015). ***Building resilience to trauma: The trauma and community resiliency models.*** New York, NY: Routledge. ISBN-10: 0415820588 ISBN-13: 978-0415820585

Levine, MD, Peter A. (1997). ***Waking the tiger: healing trauma.*** Berkeley, CA: North Atlantic Books. ISBN-10: 155643233X ISBN-13: 978-1556432330

Walker, Pete (2013). ***Complex PTSD: From surviving to thriving.*** Berkeley, CA: CreateSpace/Azure Coyote. ISBN-10: 1492871842 ISBN-13: 978-1492871842

Van der Volk, MD, Bessel (2015). ***The body keeps score: Brain, mind, and body in the healing of trauma.*** New York, NY: Penguin Books. ISBN-10: 0143127748 ISBN-13: 978-0143127741

Apps:

(Note: These are examples, not endorsements by the author.)

The Mood Meter

Headspace

iChill

Calm

Breathe2Relax

REFERENCES

American Psychiatric Association. (2013). ***Diagnostic and statistical manual of mental disorders (5th ed.).*** Washington, DC: Author.

Owens, G. (2016). Predictors of post-traumatic growth and post-traumatic stress symptom severity in undergraduates reporting potentially traumatic events. ***Journal of Clinical Psychology, 72*** (10), 1064–1076.

Shapiro, F. (2001). ***Eye movement desensitization and reprocessing (EMDR): Basic principles, protocols, and procedures (2nd ed.).*** New York, NY: The Guilford Press.

IMAGE SOURCE: IStock (Standard License)

"Whatever I have, wherever I am, I can make it through anything in the One who makes me who I am."

— Philippians 4:13

Lauren Richardson, Ph.D., MA
Laura Wingard, MA, LMFT

Addiction in Adolescents and Young Adults

The Nature of Addiction

Due to the complex nature of addiction in young people, no single definition or model for the disorder is agreed upon among mental health professionals. This is largely due to the multifaceted origin and expression of addiction. For example, some professionals emphasize biological factors (for example, genetic factors that contribute to a predisposition toward addiction). Others focus on psychological factors (such as early childhood trauma) leading to self-medication. Most practitioners, however, agree that several factors contribute to the development of addiction, and that a young person is impacted in many ways. The symptoms are all encompassing as the personhood of an addicted individual is compromised at all levels: biologically, psychologically, socially and spiritually. Thus, a common model is the biopsychosocialspiritual model—the model in use throughout this book—which takes into account the major facets of addiction's development and impact. This model focuses on the idea that addiction is a global, ongoing condition resulting from the interaction of multiple factors across domains. Additionally, within the biopsychosocialspiritual model, treatment must address all layers of impairment for the addicted young person including physical, psychological, social and spiritual health.

Another common model is the disease model. This model focuses on differences in the brain which lead to a chronic condition (DiClemente, 2018). The main idea of this model is that the brain's reward and motivation system are (or become) dysfunctional, tending to lead to a disease that impacts the person on all levels. This model is largely accepted and discussed within the Alcoholics Anonymous (AA) community. Within this model, it is often understood that the disease is something the addicted individual will always have, regardless of whether or not the person is actively using substances. Therefore, symptom management and efforts to arrest the disease process are a lifelong commitment, requiring frequent attention and care.

The disease model is further impacted by a young person's incomplete brain development. At this stage in neurological development, the portion of the brain that adults rely on to control impulses and predict the consequences of their actions, is not fully developed. The prefrontal cortex should be seen as the "voice of reason", which develops last at about age 25. Without that voice, young people tend to be more emotion driven, explorative, excitement seeking, poor with planning and judgement, and engage in risky behaviors driven by lack of impulse control. This is why we tend to see more frequent risky behaviors in young people than we do with adults. Often, young people are simply unable to control some impulses and are unable to think critically about future consequences. Much to a young person's protest, they are still dependent on healthy adults, like parents, coaches and pastors to help guide them during this time in life.

While young people do seek risky behaviors, this exploration is common and can typically be differentiated from addiction. An important distinction needs to be made between frequent substance use and addiction. Substance use, or even "problem drinking", such as frequently drinking alcohol or even regular intoxication, does not automatically indicate that an adolescent has a diagnosable addiction. While an adolescent who is regularly becoming intoxicated might need help and support, the impact of intoxication alone is not *global* and *consistent*, as with addiction. Intoxication impacts the adolescent physically and psychologically, for a brief period of time.

However, with addiction, the effects of excessive and persistent use are ongoing, often leading to physical and psychological dependence on the substance. Given this distinction, being clear how we use the term "addiction" within ministry and the church community is important.

Types of Addiction

An adolescent or young adult can become addicted to a variety of substances or behaviors, such as:

Alcohol:

Excessive and persistent use of alcohol that is characterized by physical and psychological dependence (that is, the person reports that he or she is "unable to function" without alcohol).

Drugs:

Excessive and persistent use of a substance that is characterized by physical and psychological dependence. Types of drug addictions include, but are not limited to, opioids, stimulants, hallucinogens, inhalants, sedatives/anxiolytics. As widely reported in the news, illicit drugs are not the only problem; patients can become addicted to prescription drugs as well, often moving from doctor to doctor in order to maintain access to the substance long after the medical treatment is complete.

Tobacco and Caffeine:

Excessive and persistent use of tobacco and caffeine, and failed efforts to cut back are the primary symptoms of this type of addiction. A common form of tobacco use among adolescents is through the use of e-cigarettes ("vaping"). E-cigarettes can sometimes be concealed as a household item (for example, a ballpoint pen, a USB or "thumb" drive) and can sometimes also contain liquid forms of substances other than nicotine (for example, marijuana, methamphetamine). (For more information, please see the Resources at the end of this chapter.) Caffeine can be consumed as coffee or tea, as well as in so-called "energy drinks".

Sex:

Excessive and persistent engagement in sexual thoughts and behaviors to the degree that it interferes with daily functioning. While sexual addiction has many components that differ from substance addiction, much of the information discussed within the biopsychosocialspiritual model remains applicable. (For more information, please see the Resources at the end of this chapter.) Among adolescents, this type of addiction is identified far less often than sexual compulsivity.

Gambling:

Obsessive and frequent engagement in gambling that impacts other areas of life such as relationships, school performance, and employment. Keep in mind that the gambler at a poker game is a stereotype and does not capture the full range of risky options (such as football pools, online betting, purchasing lottery tickets or visiting casinos).

Internet Gaming:

Obsessive and high frequency engagement in internet gaming in order to manage one's mood. Gaming continues despite efforts to cut back or the negative impact on relationships.

IMAGE SOURCE: Pixabay

Social Media/Smart Phone:

Similar to internet gaming, social media/ smart phone addiction, involves obsessive and high frequency engagement in several different forms of social media (Instagram, Snapchat, Twitter, etc.) in order to manage one's mood or self-worth. Despite the increased use by and negative impacts on adolescents, addiction issues related to social media and other types of internet use have not yet been recognized as a formal disorder. The reward center of the brain becomes reliant on constant external affirmation. The need for "likes" on these feeds, or a constant focus on the comments received, becomes obsessive and necessary for a young person. This can be especially harmful for young people, because they are still developing a sense of self. Similar to the example given above when discussing the difference between excessive alcohol use and alcohol addiction, it is important to remember that not all young people who excessively engage in social media have an addiction issue.

The Data

Overall, the prevalence of addiction has been either on the rise or has remained stable for the past several years. In 2018, 19.3 million Americans (7.8% of the population) over the age of 12 had an addiction to either alcohol or drugs (SAMHSA, 2018). In 2018, 9% of Americans ages 12 to 17 used alcohol, and 1.6% of Americans ages 12 to 17 had an actual addiction to alcohol. Also, in 2018, among Americans ages 12 to 17, 6.7% used marijuana and 2.1% had an actual addiction to marijuana. Marijuana addiction is on the rise, especially within the 18 to 25-year age range.

Misuse of and addiction to opioid pain killers began in the late 1990's and quickly escalated. Currently, the Centers for Disease Control and Prevention estimates that the total "economic burden" of prescription opioid misuse alone, including heroin, in the United States is $78.5 billion a year, including the costs of healthcare, lost productivity, addiction treatment, and criminal justice involvement. Among 38 states providing prescription opioid overdose death data, 17 states recently saw a documented, single-year decline between 2017-2018, and none experienced a significant increase from 2017 to 2018. Across the country, however, such overdoses continue to claim lives.

Addiction Rates Among Adolescents

In 2018, 2.8% of Americans ages 12 to 17 misused prescription pain pills, as opposed to 3.9% in 2015. Cocaine and heroin tend to be less commonly used among adolescents than among the general population, while alcohol, marijuana, stimulants and hallucinogen use tend to be more common. Cigarette use (including e-cigarettes) have the highest rate of use among adolescents. In 2019, 5.4 million adolescents regularly use cigarettes, up from 3.6 million in 2018. This increase is largely attributed to the flavored tobacco and e-cigarette industry.

Addiction issues also have a high co-occurrence rate with severe mental health issues. Examples include major depressive disorder and various types of anxiety disorders. Adolescents at higher risk for addiction issues tend to be victims of trauma or abuse, have parents who frequently use substances, have a mental health issue, or have a physical disability. In 2018, 20.3 million Americans aged 12 and older had a diagnosable addiction issue to alcohol or drugs. Despite these staggering statistics, *only 11.2% of these individuals received treatment.* And 3% of all adolescents report that they did not receive treatment for addiction issues when they needed it.

What are the Common Symptoms of Adolescent Addiction?

Addiction has a global impact on the adolescent, with various symptoms within the biological, psychological, social and spiritual domains:

Biological

- Dependence: increased physiological need for the substance
- Increased tolerance: using more of the substance to achieve the same effect
- Withdrawal symptoms: experience of negative physical symptoms when stopping the use of a substance, such that the individual will continue to use the substance in order to avoid the experience of these symptoms
- Difficulties with sleep
- Changes in appetite
- Development of other medical issues as the result of addiction (for example, liver disease in alcohol addiction)

Psychological

- Dependence: increased psychological need for the substance
- Denial of the severity of symptoms or of the need for help
- Cravings for a substance
- Considerable amount of thoughts focused on substance use and preparation for use, which is seemingly obsessive in nature
- Individual thinks that he/she needs the substance in order to get through the day
- Engaging in risky behaviors
- Anxiety
- Depression
- Mood swings
- Irritability and anger
- Restlessness

Social

- Strained or lost relationships with family and friends
- Denial of impact of addiction issues on family and friends
- Lying about substance use to family and friends
- Increased isolation
- Significant time spent with friends who also use substances or who support the adolescent's addiction
- Difficulties in school
- Legal issues (such as DUI, stealing)
- Financial issues (for example, frequently asking parents for money)
- Discontinuing activities or hobbies that the person previously enjoyed

Spiritual

- Substance becomes central focus—an idol—in an adolescent's life
- Spiritual isolation
- Spiritual despair
- Spiritual numbness
- Belief that using the substance increases a sense of peace and purpose
- Increased lack of purpose or meaning

Symptoms may vary based on the type of addiction and the substance used. You will observe the most variation within the biological domain (in other words, in the physical symptoms), because each substance has a different impact on the body and brain. (For more information on specific substance symptoms, please see the Resources section of this chapter.)

Predisposing Factors Associated with Addiction

As we've seen, addiction is a multifaceted disorder that develops as the result of many predisposing factors. An addiction is likely the result of multiple factors, such as:

- Genetic predisposition
- Family history of addiction issues
- Management of medical or physical issues through use of substance (for example, prescription pain relievers used to manage chronic pain)
- Presence of another mental health issue (such as anxiety, depression, bipolar disorder)
- Tendency to engage in high-risk behaviors
- Impulsive personality type
- Family dynamics (for example, hostility, disengagement)
- History of trauma
- History of grief and loss
- Social withdrawal, isolation
- Only "support" includes friends who also use substances
- Substance becomes center of the person's life
- Loss of resources to meet daily needs (may include food insecurity, homelessness or unstable housing, loss of financial support from family, or other factors)

Readiness for Help

Adolescents who struggle with addiction often experience a phase of denial prior to getting help. Often, family and friends are eager for the addicted person to seek help, because they have witnessed the harm and destruction caused by the adolescent's addiction. Family and friends might then put pressure on the individual to make changes or seek to do an "intervention." Parents might even find themselves wanting to step in and fix the issue for their adolescent. In other cases, parents might take the role of "enabler", by not allowing the addicted individual to experience the natural consequences of the addictive behaviors (such as legal entanglements, punishment, or loss of privileges at home or in school), or by protecting him or her from emotionally difficult or painful experiences. Rather than assume these roles, parents and other supportive individuals can instead come alongside the adolescent, to listen, validate and identify motivating factors for seeking treatment.

As a potential support to the adolescent and parent(s), youth pastors, lay leaders and educators seek to understand the adolescent and to ask questions that provoke thought about his or her values and goals. This often looks like developing a relationship with the adolescent, as the person in ministry helps the family take steps toward finding help. While parents might end up requiring treatment for their child, an addicted adolescent is likely to be more successful during treatment if he/she has identified a highly motivating factor, one that presents significantly greater benefits than the perceived benefits of substance use. Some examples of positive and negative motivating factors include:

- Future goals (such as a career or college)
- Threat to engaging in activities or hobbies (for example, not being able to play sports)
- Threat to contact with the family or support system
- Serious health issues that resulted from the addiction
- Changes in religious beliefs

In general, it is best to help the adolescent to have an active and contributing voice to the treatment process. As pastors and educators support adolescents and families in this process, they will need to manage expectations of the addicted person, as he/she might resist treatment due to lack of readiness, might need time and support to identify motivating factors, or might struggle to maintain sobriety.

Types of Treatment

Treatment often takes place in multiple phases. Additionally, commitment to recovery and sobriety often becomes a lifelong journey, thus requiring engagement in some type of maintenance program. Also, treatment is not "one size fits all". A description of various types of treatment, and ways in which the treatment might be effective for adolescents at certain points of their recovery, is provided here:

Inpatient rehabilitation or residential treatment program: This line of treatment includes immersion in 24/7 care at an inpatient treatment facility for 30 days or more. Components of treatment usually include psychotherapy (individual, family, group), psychiatry, physical health interventions, and case management. This is often the first line of treatment for adolescents who have severe addictions, or addictions that co-occur with severe mental health challenges.

Intensive outpatient program (IOP): A day treatment program that typically includes psychotherapy (individual, family, group) and psychiatry. This type of treatment is often sought by adolescents with moderate to mild forms of addiction. It is also an option that allows the adolescent to maintain academic attendance while in treatment.

12-Step program or other support group: Support groups are often the core of sobriety maintenance after an inpatient or an intensive outpatient treatment. (For examples of support groups, please see the Resources section of this chapter.)

Psychotherapy (individual, family, group): Therapy can be helpful throughout multiple phases of treatment, including the initial treatment and sobriety maintenance phases. Therapy is often incorporated for adolescents being treated for co-occurring mental health challenges.

Medication: Medication can be incorporated at multiple phases of treatment, whether to treat withdrawal symptoms while undergoing detox at initial phases of treatment, or to manage cravings and co-occurring mental health issues during sobriety maintenance.

The path of recovery is challenging and can include overcoming continued obstacles. A difficult marker of addiction recovery is the common occurrence of relapse. The rates of relapse among adolescents are generally thought to be higher than the 40% to 60% rates among adults. Therefore, as a ministry leader, it will be important to keep these rates in mind as they relate to your expectations of those in sobriety maintenance.

The 4 D's of Mental Illness

Let's summarize the information in this chapter using the 4 D's.

Deviance—How might a young person's symptoms differ from what one would normally expect to see under similar circumstances?

____

____

Dysfunction—How might a young person's experience of the disorder(s) potentially interfere with their ability to function in day-to-day life (for example, school, sports, relationship, etc.)?

____

____

Distress—Describe the biopsychosocialspiritual distress that might be associated with the disorder(s).

____

____

Danger —What types of words or actions might suggest that the young person you're interacting with is in some type of danger?

____

____

LASER

Now, use the LASER to evaluate the experiences and possible responses suggesting a more serious mental health concern.

LISTEN for key words that suggest someone may be struggling with a mental health condition

ASSESS the type and severity of the mental health issue presented

STRATEGIZE to develop a potential response to the mental health concern

EXPLORE potential interventions with the afflicted individual as well as the accessibility and openness to these options

REFER to appropriate mental health professionals when necessary

LISTEN

LISTEN for key words that suggest someone may be struggling with a mental health condition

- Sometimes I feel like I can't make it through the day without my vape pen.
- I keep asking my parents for money (to buy more drugs/alcohol).
- I can't come to the youth group event, because I want to spend some time with my other friends.
- I only spend time with my two best friends, because they understand that I need to keep smoking.
- I missed a few days school last week, because I drank too much on a weeknight.
- Taking these pills help me do better in school. I wouldn't be able to complete my assignments without them.
- I only really drink on the weekends and don't think that drinking really affects me that much.
- I can't live without my phone or gaming system.
- "My [mom, dad, teacher or sibling] is over-reacting!", or, "That coach never liked me, anyway" (or any other ways of discussing substance use that downplay its seriousness).

NOTES:

ASSESS the type and severity of the mental health issue presented

ASSESS

- Ask questions about the frequency and level of focus on substance use.
- How often do you drink, smoke, etc.?
- What drugs have you used and how often have you used them?
- Have you used an increased amount of substance over time in order to get the same affect?
- Do you experience a need for the substance in order to function, get through the day?
- How do you feel when you are not using the substance?
- Do you find yourself planning when and how you will next use the substance?

NOTES:

STRATEGIZE

STRATEGIZE to develop a potential response to the mental health concern

- Ask the adolescent about what is motivating them to use the drug. Also, discuss what other activities, such as hobbies or sports, they find motivating.
- Validate the adolescent's struggle and discuss his/her motivation to make a change.
- Assist the adolescent in identifying supportive individuals who encourage sobriety.
- Encourage parents to set firm boundaries with the adolescent.
- Explore the adolescent's perception of his/her drug use and discuss the potential or current consequences of his/her regular substance use.

NOTES:

EXPLORE potential interventions with the afflicted individual as well as the accessibility and openness to these options

EXPLORE

- Discuss treatment options with parent(s), and encourage parents to set firm boundaries with their adolescent.
- Discuss the adolescent's openness to treatment.
- Discuss motivating factors and how likely the adolescent is to accomplish his or her goals based on the motivating factors for treatment.
- Explore and validate feelings, fears and hesitations about seeking treatment.
- Encourage parent(s) to seek support (for example, therapist, pastor) in order to discern the best type of treatment for the adolescent.
- Help the adolescent and family identify treatment centers and support groups.
- Discuss potential care ministries for adolescents with addiction and/or substance use issues.

NOTES:

REFER

REFER to appropriate mental health professionals when necessary

- A referral to a treatment center would likely be the most appropriate for severe addiction. Consider guiding the parents in contacting their insurance company for a list of covered treatment facilities.
- A referral to a psychologist (Ph.D. or Psy.D.), social worker (MSW or LCSW), or marriage and family therapist (MFT) would be an appropriate referral for a mild addiction.
- You can also refer adolescents to addiction support groups.
- Parents might also benefit from a referral to a therapist as well as support groups (for example, Al-Anon).
- Regular interaction with ministry leaders allows for continued support of adolescents in treatment and/or in recovery.

NOTES:

Important Take-Aways for Ministry Leaders

- Addictions impact the adolescent on all levels, including biological, psychological, social, and spiritual.
- Substance use, even intoxication, does not automatically indicate that an adolescent has an addiction.
- The most common substances used by adolescents are alcohol, marijuana, and tobacco (through the use of e-cigarettes).
- Adolescents with addictions often have a serious mental health challenge, a history of trauma, a physical disability, a history of conflictual family dynamics, and/or parents who frequently use substances.
- Adolescents often resist treatment at first, and can benefit from supportive individuals to assist them in identifying a motivating factor for seeking help.
- Treatment includes multiple components (therapy, psychiatry, support groups, and so on) that are often provided at a treatment facility.
- Relapse is a common part of the recovery process, especially in the first year, so manage your expectations.

RESOURCES

Online Organizations and Support:

Alateen/Al-Anon (support for families/young peoples of addicted individuals): http://al-anon.org/

Alcoholic Anonymous: https://www.aa.org/

Celebrate Recovery: http://www.celebraterecovery.com/

Information on e-cigarette use among teens: https://www.cdc.gov/tobacco/basic_information/e-cigarettes/Quick-Facts-on-the-Risks-of-E-cigarettes-for-Kids-Teens-and-Young-Adults.html

Information on tobacco use among youth: https://www.cdc.gov/tobacco/data_statistics/fact_sheets/youth_data/tobacco_use/index.htm

Internet Gaming Addiction: https://www.psychiatry.org/patients-families/internet-gaming

Narcotics Anonymous: https://www.na.org/

National Institute on Drug Abuse for Teens: http://teens.drugabuse.gov/

SAMSA National Hotline: 800-662-HELP (4357)

Sex Addicts Anonymous (SAA): https://saa-recovery.org/

SMART Recovery: https://www.smartrecovery.org/teen

Substance Abuse and Mental Health Services Administration (SAMSA): http://store.samhsa.gov/list/series?name=Tips-for-Teens

Types of substance use disorders: https://www.samhsa.gov/find-help/atod

Videos:

Hanley, Megan. ***Alcohol and Drug Abuse in Teenagers:*** https://www.youtube.com/watch?v=ISMLIAXENFc

Hari, Johann. ***Everything You Thought You Knew About Addiction is Wrong:*** https://www.ted.com/talks/johann_hari_everything_you_think_you_know_about_addiction_is_wrong?language=en

Windle, Lauren. ***Lesson a Drug Addict Can Teach You:*** https://www.youtube.com/watch?v=ytVxYTavE1U

Books:

Al-Anon Family Groups (1992). ***Courage to change: One day at a time in Al-Anon II.*** Virginia Beach, VA: Al-Anon Family Group World Headquarters.

Al-Anon Family Groups (2002). ***Hope for today.*** Virginia Beach, VA: Al-Anon Family Groups World Headquarters.

Alcoholics Anonymous World Services, Inc. (1952). ***Twelve steps and twelve traditions.*** New York, NY: Author.

Franklin, K., and King, L. (2009). ***Addicted like me: a mother-daughter story of substance abuse and recovery.*** Berkeley, CA: Seal Press.

Lewis, M. (2011) ***Memoirs of an addicted brain: A neuroscientist examines his former Life on drugs.*** New York, NY: Public Affairs.

Miller, W.R., and Rollnick, S. (2012). ***Motivational interviewing: Helping people change.*** New York, NY: Guilford Press.

Narcotics Anonymous World Services (1992). ***Just for today: Daily meditations for recovering addicts (revised edition).*** Center City, MN: Hazelden Publishing.

Peele, S. (2007). ***Addiction-proof your child: A realistic approach to preventing drug, alcohol and other dependencies.*** New York, NY: Three Rivers Press.

Roberts, K. (2010). ***Cyber junkie: Escape the gaming and internet trap.*** Center City, MN: Hazelden.

Sheff, D. (2009). ***Beautiful boy: A father's journey through his son's addiction.*** New York, NY: Mariner Books

Sheff, D., and Sheff, N. (2019). ***HIGH: Everything you want to know about drugs, alcohol and addiction.*** New York, NY: Houghton Mifflin Harcourt.

Wolfe, et al. (2006). ***Adolescent risk Behaviors: Why teens experiment and strategies to keep them safe.*** Grand Rapids, MI: The Composing Room.

REFERENCES

Centers for Disease Control (May 27, 2020). ***Opioid overdose crisis.*** Retrieved from https://www.drugabuse.gov/drug-topics/opioids/opioid-overdose-crisis

Centers for Disease Control (April 16, 2020). ***Opioid summaries by state.*** Retrieved from https://www.drugabuse.gov/drug-topics/opioids/opioid-summaries-by-state

DiClemente, C. C. (2018). ***Addiction and change: How addictions develop and addicted people recover (2nd ed.)*** New York, NY: Guilford Press.

Substance Abuse and Mental Health Services Administration (2014). ***Gender differences in primary substance of abuse across age groups.*** Retrieved from https://www.samhsa.gov/data/sites/default/files/sr077-gender-differences-2014.pdf

Substance Abuse and Mental Health Services Administration (2018). ***National survey on drug use and health.*** Retrieved from https://www.samhsa.gov/data/data-we-collect/nsduh-national-survey-drug-use-and-health

IMAGE SOURCE: Shutterstock (Standard License)

"I praise you because I am fearfully and wonderfully made;
your works are wonderful, I know that full well."

— Psalm 139:14

Angela Hanford, Ph.D.

Eating Disorders in Adolescents and Young Adults

The Nature of Eating Disorders in Adolescents and Young Adults

The adolescent and young adult years are a time of great cognitive and emotional growth, including identity development. Although Psalm 139 reminds us of our value as God's creations, this time can still be a period of insecurity and self-comparisons. It is no surprise that eating disorders and body image struggles are common during this time of life. It does not help that today's adolescents and young adults are bombarded with images and statements throughout social media and the internet that focus on body comparisons and an ideal body, along with bullying and shaming of certain body shapes and sizes.

People who struggle with disordered eating or body image concerns may or may not have a diagnosable eating disorder. Skipping breakfast or lunch to avoid the extra calories would be an example of disordered eating. These "subclinical" presentations, which are statistically more common, still result in emotional distress and can have an impact on one's body, functioning, and interpersonal relationships. Someone who cycles through diets may experience deep feelings of shame and body hatred, yet not meet criteria for a diagnosable eating disorder.

To understand eating disorders, it is important to realize that eating disorders are not simply about losing weight, food, or even appearance. We can see this in anorexia nervosa (AN) when an extremely low body weight does not result in body satisfaction, but in continued starvation. In fact, someone who has an eating disorder may not know who they are, and may struggle with intense feelings of shame and the belief that he or she is not good enough. The compensatory behaviors, such as starvation or purging, may be the only way that an individual knows how to cope with chaotic emotions and life.

Unless these underlying hurts are addressed, the eating disorder behavior will not resolve. Therefore, it is important for people to realize that telling someone to "just eat more", or asking, "Don't you know that you are hurting yourself?" will not be sufficient. Rather, someone with an eating disorder needs support, empathy, and love as he

Figure 1
Measuring Tape and Scale for Tracking Weight

IMAGE SOURCE: Pixabay

or she journeys toward recovery. Furthermore, eating disorders can have a severe impact on physical health, as well as on every aspect of one's life, making accurate assessment and treatment critical.

Types of Eating Disorders

The *Diagnostic and Statistical Manual of Mental Disorders (5th ed.)*, or DSM-5, defines eight types of "feeding and eating disorders", all based on specific criteria that must be met in order to diagnose (American Psychiatric Association, 2013). In the context of ministry, anorexia nervosa, bulimia nervosa, binge-eating disorder (BED), and other specified feeding or eating disorders are the diagnoses most likely to be observed. All the information presented is in the following descriptions is based on criteria defined in the DSM-5 (American Psychiatric Association, 2013).

Anorexia Nervosa (AN):

The person restricts food intake to the point that he or she has significantly low body weight. Food restriction for children and teenagers may result in failure to develop or to gain appropriate weight. There is also an extreme fear regarding weight gain, and/or the individual may use behaviors to prevent weight gain (for example, diuretics or excessive exercise). He or she often has a distorted view of body weight or body shape, and may deny the seriousness of the symptoms. Self-esteem may also be highly influenced by perceived body size and shape. There are two types of AN: restricting type or binge-eating/purging type. The restricting type is diagnosed when an individual limits food intake and/or exercises excessively, while the binge-eating or purging type involves binging on large amounts of food or drink, followed by purging (for example, vomiting, diuretic use). (Please see the bulimia nervosa section for further definition).

Bulimia Nervosa (BN):

Bulimia nervosa occurs when someone frequently binge eats, and then subsequently engages in a behavior that is meant to prevent weight gain (for example, vomiting, laxative, excessive exercise, diuretic use). A binge is more than simply "emotional eating." When binging occurs, a very large amount of food is consumed, and there is a feeling of being out of control while eating. Someone with BN also places a high degree of emphasis on body shape in self-evaluation.

Binge Eating Disorder (BED):

This diagnosis occurs when someone has frequent episodes of binge eating, which are very distressing to the individual. Along with a larger than typical amount of food consumption, someone with BED has at least three other symptoms such as:

- eating to the point of feeling uncomfortably full,
- eating quickly,
- continuing to eat even though not hungry,
- feeling upset with oneself after binging behavior, or
- eating alone due to feelings of embarrassment of portion size.

This type of binging behavior often results in significant shame, causing many people to hide their disordered eating behaviors from others.

Pica:

A person diagnosed with pica will frequently eat items that are not food and, therefore, do not have nutritional value, such as dirt or paper. During diagnosis, the professional will take into account the individual's developmental level (for example, an infant eating dirt while playing would not be considered to have pica), and whether what is ingested is typical for his or her culture. Most cases of pica occur in conjunction with other conditions. For example, individuals who have an intellectual disability, autism spectrum disorder, or another medical condition (for example, pregnancy or brain damage) might engage in pica-like of behavior without receiving that diagnosis. In such cases, pica is diagnosed only when it is severe and needs additional, specific treatment.

Rumination Disorder:

This diagnosis is given when someone regurgitates food on a consistent basis, but the behavior is not due to any medical condition. The food could be spit out or re-chewed, for instance, but the main characteristic is that it is regurgitated.

Avoidant/Restrictive Food Intake Disorder (ARFID):

When a person has ARFID, he or she avoids or restricts food intake to the point of nutritional deficits, as evidenced by weight loss. Unlike AN or BN, there are no body image concerns fueling the restriction. An example of ANFID would be a child who has difficulty eating due to food texture, ends up losing a significant amount of weight and, as a result, has growth problems. In addition, the diagnosis would not be given if the restriction was due to lack of food access, a medical condition, or a cultural practice, such as fasting.

Other Specified Feeding or Eating Disorder (OSFED):

This diagnosis is used when symptoms of an eating disorder are present, resulting in distress and impairment, but they do not necessarily meet criteria for another diagnosis. For example, someone may have all the symptoms of AN except for low enough weight. Another example may be someone who binges and purges, but not frequently enough for a diagnosis of BN. Both of these instances may still be significant enough to require treatment. Orthorexia, for instance, could also be a presentation of OSFED. The term "orthorexia" has been used to describe a fixation on eating healthy food (Bratman & Knight, 2000, pg. 9). Although this may sound positive, someone who is very fixated and controlling could experience significant distress about eating, or could develop deficits in nutrition and various medical problems.

The Data

Eating disorders, specifically AN, BN, and BED, often emerge during adolescence or young adulthood (APA, 2013). Prevalence rates for anorexia nervosa (AN) have been reported as 0.3% to 1% in young adult females by the Academy for Eating Disorders (AFED), whereas rates for bulimia nervosa (BN) were 1% to 3% for the same population (AFED, 2017). Adolescent participants in the National Comorbidity Survey Replication Adolescent Supplement (NCS-A), a mental health survey of over 9,000 adolescents in the United States, reported a lifetime prevalence of 0.3% for AN, 0.9% for BN, and 1.6% for BED (Swanson, et. al, 2011). One interesting note in this study is that the majority of respondents had not received treatment for their eating disorders.

It is important to remember that most disordered eating and body image concerns do not meet diagnostic criteria for an eating disorder, yet they can still have significant consequences. In fact, studies have shown that rates of eating disordered behavior are higher than diagnosable eating disorders, with a 14% to 22% prevalence rate (Jones, Bennett, Olmsted, Lawson, & Rodein, 2001; Holling & Schlack, 2007). The incidence rates are higher if disordered eating and body image concerns are also included. When these concerns are added, studies have shown, the rates of disordered eating behavior in general (22%) are higher than the rate of only diagnosable eating disorders alone (14%) (Jones, Bennett, Olmsted, Lawson, & Rodein, 2001; Holling & Schlack, 2007). This highlights the importance of recognizing that disordered eating behavior, regardless of whether it exists in the context of a diagnosable disorder, occurs frequently and needs attention.

What are the Common Symptoms of an Adolescent Eating Disorder?

Following are some symptoms suggesting that someone might be struggling with an eating disorder, a sub-clinical eating disorder, or a body image disturbance. In contrast, it's also possible that someone might display a symptom or symptoms and yet not be experiencing an eating disorder.

Physical

- Frequent self-criticism of one's body and/or eating behaviors (or those of others)
- Fixation on calorie intake or calories burned
- Significant weight loss or weight gain
- Frequent dieting
- Skipping meals
- Swollen cheeks (indicating swollen lymph nodes from vomiting)
- Wearing baggy clothes
- Lethargy
- Stomachache, nausea
- Frequently throwing up

Psychological

- Mood swings: depression, anxiety, irritability
- Intrusive thoughts about body image or food
- Self-hatred and/or body hatred
- Feeling like one is "not good enough"

Social

- Isolation; avoiding or pulling away from relationships
- Avoiding social gatherings revolving around food
- Bringing own food to social events
- Embarrassment or shame when eating in front of others

Spiritual

- Pulling away from God
- Fear of God being angry
- Shame before God
- A sense of being bad or not good enough
- Insecurity regarding God

Risk Factors for Eating Disorders

Eating disorders are complex and do not have only one single, known cause. As we look at risk factors for eating disorders, it is important to understand that a risk factor is not necessarily a ***cause***. In addition, in keeping with our biopsychosocialspiritual model, many factors likely play a role in someone developing an eating disorder. The following is a list of factors that have been associated with eating disorders:

Biological/Genetic: For example, having a close relative who has an eating disorder is a risk factor for developing an eating disorder (APA, 2013). Females also have more reported eating disorders than do males (APA, 2013)

Frequent Dieting: Dieting promotes an emphasis on a certain weight and body size, which can lead to someone developing an eating disorder. Not everyone who diets has an eating disorder; however, frequent dieting does suggest, at minimum, distress over body image. It can also affect metabolism and health in the longer term.

Trauma: This includes sexual abuse, physical abuse, and verbal abuse, along with other types of trauma.

Temperament/Psychological: Examples include perfectionism, feeling a lack of control over one's life and/or emotions, depression, anxiety, substance abuse, low self-esteem, and difficulty coping with and expressing emotions.

Environment/Family: A history of bullying or being teased, especially about appearance, can contribute to body image struggles Some family dynamics that have been associated with eating disorders include a chaotic family, emotionally disconnection, rigidity, an emphasis on physical appearance, and being overly critical. *(Note that research has not demonstrated that family dynamics are the sole cause of an eating disorder. However, family environments can be risk factors for disordered eating behavior. In addition, family dynamics are an important component for consideration in treatment of eating disorders.)*

Culture/Society: For example, Western society's focus on a desirable body type, whether it be the very slim female ideal or the muscular, hyper-masculine body, may contribute to body dissatisfaction.

Media/Internet: This can often be seen in the media's use of computer enhanced bodies and faces. Many teens and young adults are susceptible because they are not aware of this phenomenon (see, for example, the short video by *The Dove Self-Esteem Foundation* at https://www.youtube.com/watch?v=iYhCn0jf46U).

Sports: Sports that promote a certain weight or body size are more prone to eating disorders and body image struggles. These include, for example, dance, wrestling, swimming, and gymnastics.

Careers: Careers with a focus on physical appearance, such as acting and modeling, may also contribute to body dissatisfaction and eating disorder behavior.

Special Considerations

Males

Eating disorders are commonly associated with females. Statistically, females do have a higher prevalence of eating disorders (APA, 2013). That being said, however, it is important to remember that males can also develop eating disorders with the potential for equally severe consequences. For instance, consider the wrestler who starves himself, purges, or even exercises to the point of exhaustion to "make weight" before a match, then competes intensely while in a weakened state. Due to the association of eating disorders with females in our society, males may even experience added shame when admitting that they need help.

Medical Complications

Since eating disorders can have significant, life-threatening medical complications, early intervention and treatment are vital. Health complications vary based on diagnosis, but can include such things as heart problems, dehydration, blood pressure fluctuations, organ problems, hypothermia, menstrual irregularities, delay of puberty, bone density loss, esophageal tears, digestive problems, and depression (APA, 2013). Although these are but a few of the possible medical complications resulting from eating disorders, they highlight the vital necessity of medical treatment.

Suicide

Although not everyone who has an eating disorder is actively suicidal, it bears noting that there can be a risk for suicide in those who have an eating disorder diagnosis. Specifically, research has shown that there is an increased suicide risk for those diagnosed with AN and BN compared to the general population (APA, 2013; Pompili, Giradi, Tatarelli, Ruberto, & Tatarelli, 2006). Therefore, it is important to do an assessment of suicide risk when working with anyone who has an eating disorder (please see chapter on depression and suicide for more information)

IMAGE SOURCE: Pixabay

The Internet and Social Media

Although the internet and social media can offer helpful resources for understanding eating disorders and eating disorder recovery, both can also be very triggering. For example, seeing an Instagram post full of women posing in swimsuits, or a posting of weight loss "successes" can be very triggering for someone who is struggling with body image and eating disorders. Moreover, sites that are pro-anorexia or pro-eating disorder, which actually promote an eating disorder mindset and accompanying behaviors, can also trigger a reaction. It is very important to be educated about eating disorder triggers on the internet and social media, as these are frequent sources of stress for those suffering from these disorders.

The 4 D's of Mental Illness

Let's summarize the information in this chapter using the 4 D's.

Deviance—How might a person's symptoms differ from what one would normally expect to see under similar circumstances?

____

____

Dysfunction—How might a person's experience of the disorder(s) potentially interfere with their ability to function in day-to-day life (e.g., work, relationship, etc.)?

____

____

Distress—Describe the biopsychosocialspiritual distress that might be associated with the disorder(s).

____

____

Danger —What types of words or actions might suggest that the person you're interacting with is in some type of danger?

____

____

LASER

Now, use the LASER to evaluate the experiences and possible responses suggesting a more serious mental health concern.

LISTEN for key words that suggest someone may be struggling with a mental health condition

ASSESS the type and severity of the mental health issue presented

STRATEGIZE to develop a potential response to the mental health concern

EXPLORE potential interventions with the afflicted individual as well as the accessibility and openness to these options

REFER to appropriate mental health professionals when necessary

LISTEN

LISTEN for key words that suggest someone may be struggling with a mental health condition

- Frequent critical comments: "I hate my body", "I'm so fat", "Am I that fat..."
- "I can't eat this because it has too many calories"
- "I need to skip breakfast because I ate too much last night"
- "I'm nervous to eat in front of people"
- "Listen" with not only your ears but with your eyes, for behaviors that may suggest an eating disorders (for example, pushing food around plate without eating much, skipping meals, consistently visiting the restroom after eating).

NOTES:

ASSESS the type and severity of the mental health issue presented

ASSESS

- Basic assessment questions to determine if there is an eating disorder:
  - Have you been restricting food intake?
  - Do you make yourself throw up in order to avoid gaining weight?
  - Do you exercise to avoid gaining weight? If so, how much?
  - How long has this been going on?
- What might be triggering the disordered eating behavior?
- Do you notice any medical complications (for example, dehydration)?
- Are suicidal thoughts present?
- Are other conditions present, such as depression, anxiety, substance use or abuse, self-harm behaviors?
- Does the individual have appropriate social support?
- How (or are) family members involved?

NOTES:

STRATEGIZE

STRATEGIZE to develop a potential response to the mental health concern

- Consider what treatment options are available in your area, such as therapists, medical doctors, support groups, psychiatrists, or dietitians. Be careful when recommending support groups, as some groups focus on dieting or eating habits, which may perpetuate the eating disorder mindset.
- Determine what behaviors are harmful or helpful for the individual (for example, family member responses).
- Explore current life stressors and ways to cope with or cut out stressors.
- Does the individual have people who he or she trusts for emotional support?
- What could interfere with seeking help?
- Discuss to talk to and support spouse and other family members about these issues.

NOTES:

EXPLORE potential interventions with the afflicted individual as well as the accessibility and openness to these options

EXPLORE

- Explore willingness to participate in treatment, including any fears and ambivalence to eating disorder recovery.
- Examine how to best support the individual during the recovery process (for example, one-on-one sessions, appropriate small groups for spiritual/social support, or family support/support groups).
- Consider what to do when individuals will not seek support.
- Explore ways to help the family access treatment and support options.

NOTES:

REFER

REFER to appropriate mental health professionals when necessary

- Eating disorders are treatable.
- Make referrals for assessment: to a psychologist/therapist who specializes in the treatment of eating disorders and also to a medical doctor.
- Other referrals that will likely be made:
  - Dietitian who specializes in eating disorder treatment.
  - Psychiatrist for medication evaluation.
- If suicidal thoughts are present, provide emergency guidance, including a hospital for acute suicidality, crisis lines, or call 9-1-1.
- If the eating disorder is severe, discuss how the family feels about higher levels of care (for example, inpatient, residential, or intensive outpatient)

NOTES:

Important Take-Aways for Ministry Leaders

- Eating disorders, disordered eating behavior, and body image struggles are common in adolescents and young adults and can have serious consequences (for example, medical complications).
- Sub-clinical presentations of eating disorders are more common, and also impact one's life and may require treatment.
- Early intervention can be a key to a better long-term prognosis.
- Eating disorders are not just about food or losing weight, but have deep roots such as shame and not feeling good enough.
- Common disordered eating behaviors include severe restriction of food intake, purging behaviors (for example, vomiting, using diuretics), and/or binge eating.
- Although there are a variety of risk factors, eating disorders are complex and do not have one single cause.
- There is a heightened risk of suicidal thinking compared to the general population.
- The shame involved with an eating disorder is often reflected in one's relationship with God. For example, the person may feel as though God is mad at him, or that God will not accept her.
- Treatment is possible, and it usually includes a psychotherapist, medical doctor, dietitian, and, sometimes, a psychiatrist.

RESOURCES

Online Organizations and Support:

The Academy for Eating Disorders: aedweb.org

International Association of Eating Disorders Professionals: iadep.com

National Eating Disorder Association: nationaleatingdisorders.org

National Institute of Mental Health: nimh.hih.gov/index.shtml

National Suicide Prevention Lifeline: suicidepreentionlifeline.org

The Meadows Ranch: meadowsranch.com

Timberline Knolls Residential Treatment Center: timberlineknolls.com

Videos:

Dying to Be Thin (Produced by NOVA and PBS): https://www.pbs.org/video/nova-dying-to-be-thin/

Books:

Morrow, J. (2013). ***Hope for the hollow: A thirty-day inside-out makeover for women recovering from eating disorders.*** Raleigh, NC: Lighthouse Publishing of the Carolinas. ISBN-10: 1938499271 ISBN-13: 978-1938499272

Muhlheim, L. (2018). ***When your teen has an eating disorder: Practical strategies to help your teen recover from anorexia, bulimia, and binge eating.*** Oakland, CA: New Harbinger Publications. ISBN-13: 978-1684030439

Schaefer, J. (2009). ***Goodbye Ed, hello Me: Recover from your eating disorder and fall in love with life.*** New York, NY: McGraw-Hill. ISBN-10: 1938499271 ISBN-13: 978-1938499272

Schaefer, J., and Rutledge, T. (2003). ***Life without Ed: How one woman declared independence from her eating disorder and how you can, too.*** New York, NY: McGraw-Hill. ISBN-10: 0071422986 ISBN-13: 978-0071422987

Crisis Hotlines:

National Suicide Prevention Lifeline: 800-273-TALK
National Hopeline Network: 800-SUICIDE
Suicide Prevention Crisis Hotline: 877-7CRISIS

Apps:

(Note: Be careful when suggesting apps that track food and exercise unless they have been recommended by a dietitian or therapist, as the content can trigger someone struggling with eating disorder behavior. Instead, focus more on apps that help with coping skills and learning to track feelings.)

CBT Companion: Allows users to track mood and thoughts

CBT Thought Diary: For tracking emotions and thoughts

DBT Coach: Tracking of mood and use of DBT Skills

Mindfulness apps (for example, ***CALM, Headspace, Abide***)

What's Up?: Tracks feelings and thoughts, coping skill, and information about depression and anxiety

REFERENCES

Academy For Eating Disorders (2017). ***Fast facts on eating disorders: How common are eating disorders?*** Retrieved from https://www.aedweb.org/learn/resources/fast-facts#8.

American Psychiatric Association. (2013). ***Diagnostic and statistical manual of mental disorders (5th ed.).*** Washington, DC: Author.

Bratman S., Knight, D. (2000). ***Health food junkies. Orthorexia nervosa: Overcoming the obsession with healthful eating.*** New York, NY: Broadway.

Holling, H., & Schlack, R. (2007). Eating disorders in children and adolescents. First results of the German health interview and examination survey for children and adolescents. ***Bundesgesundheitsblatt, Gesundheitsforschung, Gesundheitsschutz, 50***(5-6), 794-799.

Jones, J.M., Bennett, S., Olmsted, M.P., Lawson, M.L., & Rodin, G. (2001). Disordered eating attitudes and behaviors in teenaged girls: A school-based study. ***Canadian Medical Association Journal, 65***(5), 457-552.

Pompili, M., Girardi, P., Tatarelli, G., Ruberto, A., & Tatarelli, R. (2006). Suicide and attempted suicide in eating disorders, obesity and weight-image concern. ***Eating Behaviors, 7***(4), 384-394.

Swanson, S.A., Crow, S.J., Le Grange, D., Swendesen, J., & Merikangas, K.R. (2011). Prevalence and correlates of eating disorders in adolescents: Results from the national comorbidity survey replication adolescent supplement. ***Archives of General Psychiatry, 68***(7), 714-723.

About the Editors

Kevin Van Lant is a licensed, clinical psychologist who received his Ph.D. from Rosemead School of Psychology. Kevin serves as the director of CIFT Equip and maintains a clinical practice at the Center for Individual and Family Therapy (CIFT). Kevin is also a full-time professor at Biola University where he teaches graduate courses in pastoral counseling, mental health and the church, and marriage counseling. He works primarily with depression, anxiety, trauma and those suffering from long-term emotional and spiritual distress. Kevin speaks on a broad range of topics including men's issues, parenting, marriage, and general dynamics within all relationships. He also trains pastors, educators and lay-leaders on triaging common mental health issues using the Frontlines approach included in this manual.

Laura Wingard received both her Master's in Theology and Master's in Psychology from Fuller Theological Seminary. Laura spent many years in youth ministry and is currently a practicing licensed marriage and family therapist at the Center for Individual and Family Therapy.

Made in the USA
Las Vegas, NV
03 December 2021